God's Odds
Pascal's Wager Revisited

Second Edition

J.C.W. West

Foreword by
The Right Reverend Alden Hathaway

St. Catherine's Press   stcatherinespress.com

St. Catherine's Press

www.stcatherinespress.com

A set of books in preparation:

Academic Legends in Biblical Theology

Volume I: Biblical Legends: A Philosophical Overture
Volume II: Abraham, Moses and the Missing Clay Tablets
Volume III: The Isaiah Conspiracy
Volume IV: The Daniel Hoax
Volume V: The Gospel Truth: A More Likely Scenario
Volume VI: Hiding in Plain Sight: *Logos* and *Logia*

ISBN 978-0615611419

Second edition February 2013

The cover picture is from a painting by
the poet and artist William Blake (1757 – 1827)

To my fellow Pilgrims, Table Workers,
Rectors, Rectoras, Administrators, Cha-chas and Chaplains
in the Cursillo, Walk to Emmaus, Anglican Fourth Day,
Via de Cristo, Unidos in Cristo, Kairos,
Presbyterian Pilgrimage, Great Banquet,
Credo Recovery, Chrysalis Community,
Encounter Christ, and other versions of
The Little Course,
with joy and fellowship

Contents

Foreword

The informal house parties at the West cottage on the Gulf coast of Florida welcome interesting friends and acquaintances and visitors passing through. The gatherings typically become spontaneous, extended, free-wheeling, delightfully stimulating conversations, punctuated by good food and drink, long walks on the beach, a little Latin rhythm on the steel drum, and board games (the competition is fierce), and short naps, as needed or desired. Nothing is off limits in the talk—politics, religion, science, music, literature, current events and local gossip, philosophy and theology—but always tethered and grounded in the gospel of Christ. Reading *God's Odds* reminds me of those precious symposiums by the sea.

"Perhaps the time is ripe," wrote the French theologian Etienne Gilson in his Foreword to the 1958 edition to Augustine's 'The City of God', "to recall the age-old metaphysical principle, that the only force capable of preserving a thing is the force which created it." Now fifty-four years later the time could not be riper. Our self-congratulatory secular age wants us all to believe that we can have all the goods without the need for God, or anything beyond ourselves. But we are beginning to become suspicious that there is no way that we can continue to enjoy the liberal fruits of our Judeo Christian cultural heritage if we would disdain or qualify the root convictions that have produced them. It's time to take another look at the old, old story.

It's a matter of first principles. "In the beginning was the Word" wrote the evangelist, "and the Word was God. And the word became flesh and dwelt among us". The ecumenical and missionary pioneer Bishop Lesslie Newbigin taught that there is no science, world-view, plausibility structure or philosophy that can satisfactorily explain the resurrection of Jesus of Nazareth from the dead—except that for which it is the first article of our belief. For to hold that the risen Jesus is the primary reason underlying all truth and the first premise for all understanding, is to trust that the promises of God are true. It is thus to see the world in an entirely different light—and to see our lives within it as a radically different game to be played. Halleluia, Christ is Risen.

Ultimately it is a matter of faith—or to put it more directly, an intellectual wager: a bet to be gambled. "Play the game for more than you can afford to lose," said Winston Churchill. "... only then will you learn the game." It is just what West is challenging us to do by this little book.

West draws on an idea from the French enlightenment philosopher and mathematician Blaise Pascal (1623-1662). Pascal was one of the first scholars to make a systematic study of chance and choice and probability theory. He also became a convinced Christian and in a short essay entitled 'The Wager' he proposed the idea that there was enough probable cause to believe the claims of the gospel to be valid and true and that betting ones reason, and therefore one's life on them, was eminently worthy of faith.

In a style that is breezy and informal, conversational and anecdotal, philosophical and technical (we appreciate that West has been a teacher of philosophy and literature), our author leads us on excursions into music and art (West is an accomplished pianist and composer), and discusses the physics of astronomy and the biology of brain physiology in near death experience of life beyond life, yet with the open wonder of true science.

But the fertile field here is the rich harvest of biblical study, and the teaching of the one holy catholic and apostolic Church. West unfolds for us a cursory yet comprehensive review of the faith once delivered to the saints from the perspective of the Anglican heritage.

West's book is an easy and enjoyable read. Beautiful Dreamers (whom we meet in the book) may fight it all the way, and they may wonder why it goes where it goes. But the intellectual ride is well worth the trip. The fascination engendered by this sometimes tongue-in-cheek reasoning will stimulate your own. It should persuade you to make your wager on the odds of God with more rational evidence and self-knowledge than before your encounter. The odds are that you may learn 'The Game of Life in Christ'; and hope for the ongoing work of God that is the redemption of the world.

God's Odds makes a case for the orthodox Christian Faith; a proposition that our typical twenty-first century man or woman in the street can get her mind around—a vision that can move his heart

+Alden Hathaway
Resigned Episcopal Bishop of Pittsburgh

Idiosyncrasies

Footnotes and end notes:
Footnotes at the bottom of the pages[1] are comments on the text. End notes with lower case Roman numerals[i] are citations of the sources of information. This separation is my own idiosyncrasy because finding end notes interrupts my train of thought, sometimes only later to discover that some of them have interesting comments . . . but by then I have forgotten what the context was. I hope the reader does not find this arrangement distracting.

Style. I consider it illogical to put punctuation inside quotation marks and parentheses willy-nilly, whether or not the punctuation is proper to the quotation or parenthetical. Hence periods and question marks are often found outside a quotation or parenthetical.

Double quotation marks, "x", are used for direct quotations, whether from written material, or actual or fictional quotation of speech. The punctuation of the sentence in which it appears is never used inside the quotation marks that set it off from that sentence.

Single quotation marks, or inverted commas, 'x', are used to indicate a term or word or phrase that is under discussion, and biblical authors as author. The punctuation of the sentence in which it appears is never used inside the inverted commas.

Italics, *x*, are used to set off foreign words or phrases, and the titles of books, including the titles of books in the Bible.

---

[1] Like this. See how easy it is to read a footnote?

Scare quotes are double quotation marks used to emphasize a word or phrase, and sometimes used to substitute for the phrase 'so-called'. They are bad form according to a prejudice I inherited from a former professor,[2] and are used only in desperation or defiance.

Square brackets [x] indicate my own insertions into what is otherwise someone else's discussion or opinion.

[2] Professor John Mulhern, formerly of the Philosophy faculty of Bryn Mawr College.

1.
God's Odds

Christianity isn't a philosophy, a set of ideas.
It isn't a path of spirituality. It isn't a rule of life.
It isn't a political agenda.
It includes and indeed gives energy to all those things;
but at its very heart it is something different.
It is good news about
an event which has happened in the world,
an event because of which
the world can never be the same again.
And those who believe it and live by it
will never be the same again either

N.T. Wright [ii]

But is there a God at the heart of Christianity?

Christianity may in all probability be good news for the world, as N.T. Wright points out here. But Christianity itself may not be good news if it is not undergirded by what Blaise Pascal refers to as "the God of Abraham, Isaac, and Jacob, the God and Father of our Lord Jesus Christ"

What are the odds that Pascal's God made the universe? Poor to none? Is believing in God's existence a stupid bet for us as individuals? Or are God's odds so overwhelming that we'd better put our money on him?

➢ Either there is a God who made our universe and everything else, or there is no such being.

> ➤ What if we bet that God does not exist? We have a fifty-fifty chance of being right, don't we?

No. It only *seems* to be a fifty-fifty chance. If there are fifty-two cards in a normal deck of cards, and you draw a card, it is either the jack of diamonds or not the jack of diamonds. But it is obvious to any idiot that the odds of drawing the jack of diamonds are not fifty-fifty. Drawing a not-the-jack is much more probable. There are fifty-one other cards in that deck – and quite a few more cards in God's deck, too.

The present discussion focuses on the subject matter of a short essay by the French Enlightenment philosopher Blaise Pascal ("Blĕz Pas-**cal'**"). Instead of the questions of whether or not there *is* a God, or the *nature* of God's existence, we focus here on the *odds* of God's existing— is there a God or not?—and the very practical issue of *how we should bet*.

Nor do we probe deeply here into the mathematics of probability, which remain a dark mystery to the author. There is plenty of fodder for discussion at the level a former English major can understand. I can handle a fifty-fifty chance, and astronomical odds. Between those is a dangerous cloud for me, and I don't venture into trying to discuss what it hides.

The physics of Heisenbergian indeterminacy is said to imply that it is not only we who are taking bets on God's existence, but that the universe itself is a gamble—God as creator, as it were, gambling with the universe. Einstein, on the other hand, is rumored to have assured us that God doesn't play dice.

God's alternative to leaving things to chance is simple: Cheat. That is to say, construct your own universe, just like you want it! Sidestep chance completely. Make a universe from scratch. How? Just speak it into existence. You might even, if you can do it, create its inhabitants in such a way that they can be aware of your existence as their creator. Make them to love you and worship you. One step more wonderful than that: make them so they have a choice to love you or **not** to love you and worship you. And then inspire them to love you, in spite of the odds.

Who can speak things into existence, and make it actually happen? In *The Mind of the Maker*, the mystery writer Dorothy Sayers gives an analogy that both sheds light on the creative process and obscures the distinction between novelist and Creator. She attests to the seeming free will of the characters she creates in her novels. But she glides past the distinction between the very limited character in a novel and the flesh-and-blood-and-soul person that she herself is—made by the mind of the maker and spoken into actual flesh-and-blood   existence.

This distinction is implicitly executed in a book I read some time ago and have lost, about a little girl who is a character in a novel. Her life consists only of episodes in the novel. She has no knowledge of anything not in those episodes. Walking along the beach some months ago I was struck by the impossibility of describing a real, living person. Even the seemingly simple act of taking one step entails so many inner workings of the human body, so many social workings of the human community, and so many idiomatic workings of the human soul (whatever that is) that a long, boring book would be needed (and would fail) to describe only one step along the beach, much less an entire person. And even then its entirety cannot be described—much less created—by the human author. The creatures of our authorial minds are poor shadows of the creatures we actually are. The Creator is an intelligence whose very speaking causes the planets to run in their orbits and the Krebs cycle to run in our bodies. Without him nothing would be anything at all.

Consider entropy. Recall the singularity that gets Big Banged into kajillions of proto-atoms. Recall the law of entropy from high school physics? Isaac Asimov points out, "All you have to do is nothing and everything deteriorates, collapses, breaks down and wears out , all by itself – and that is what the Second Law [of Thermodynamics] is all about." [iii] That's entropy.

Entropy says that matter in a closed system tends toward chaos. If it starts chaotic, it stays chaotic. It doesn't naturally organize itself into complex systems such as stars and planets, much less into plants, animals, and Political Science Departments. Organization requires outside intervention, design, maintenance, gardening, creativity, and someone doing the laundry. This universe meets those requirements: we're here.

The Creator cannot be merely part of His own universe. A novelist cannot be part of his own book. He could write a character into his novel, and call him by his own name, but even in an autobiography the character is less than a whole person. Any story, no matter how long and boring, is less than the actuality. Remember my attempt to describe a single step.

Just as the novelist has more dimensions, and is greater in sheer quantity of information than any of his characters could possibly be, the Creator would have to be greater than matter, more brilliant and powerful, to have spoken material things into existence. And he has devised ways to communicate with his creatures—us—to tell us about himself and about what he wants us to do. Perhaps he was bored at the idea (we gratuitously attribute motives to him) of making a universe of creatures designed simply to love him and worship him and to do nothing else, so he gave us the ability to refuse to worship him.

If anyone wants to hypothesize that there are more universes than ours, go ahead. With a leap of faith beyond any evidence,[3] we can imagine that the Creator is brilliant enough so that he can have spoken into being many universes: one in pastels, one in oils, one in the key of G#, one in the key of d minor, each with a different choreography. We can have no knowledge of them at all, unless He gives us inklings of them. In poetry, I assume. Set to music, surely. We can only know what our maker allows us to know about himself and about our own universe—and we haven't reached the end of that yet, by a long stretch. So what are the odds that he exists? Excellent. If we exist, he exists.

---

[3] Except that if he was brilliant enough to create one universe, it seems to follow that if he wanted to, he could create others as well.

Of course it's not quite that simple. So let's not end the discussion there. A First Cause is not a reason to bet that we should believe even in the Jewish God, the God of Abraham, Isaac, and Jacob, much less the Christian God, who is the Jewish God in spades—as Pascal says, "the God and Father of our Lord Jesus Christ".[iv] So Pascal has set the bar high for the wager.

Consider all four possibilities:

1.God exists and we bet that he exists.	2.God exists and we bet that he does not exist.
3.God does not exist and we bet that he exists.	4.God does not exist and we bet that he does not exist.

At first glance, it looks like the only way for Christianity to win is for God to exist, and for us to bet on his existence: That is, Christianity has a one in four chance. Not very good odds. But that is deceptive. Actually, given the evidence, as we shall see below, Christianity has a four out of four chance. Pretty good chance, eh? We're not here trying to bet on the propositional truth of whether or not God exists, but on winning the pragmatic prize: the greatest amount of personal pleasure. This is a practical wager—what will get us the most goodies? But even if we were betting on truth, it is easy to see that God's odds would be enormously favorable.

The reason to suggest a pragmatic pleasure distinction is to point out that this is not like a poker game. In poker we bet on what cards are where, and if we win, we get poker chips. Ugh! Only after we cash in our chips do we get the cash jackpot. And then, what is cash until we buy with it something such as food or shelter or music or books or camaraderie that give us real pleasure? Unlike poker, the bet here is more like a game in amateur sports, such as tennis or golf, where the very playing of the game is part of the reward. Or it is a game more like paper, rock and scissors,[4] with the penalty flowing directly from the loss. But then I should point out that it is also a team sport, where a good portion of the fun is in interacting with the other players. Whatever it is, we are playing to win, we are betting for keeps—"for keepers", as our childhood games of marbles often were. It is a game of skill, like marbles, but I argue here that the skill is not our own. We are betting on someone else's expertise. And unlike betting on professional basketball or football, our player's skill is completely calculable. We just have to comprehend how immense his skill is, and our bet is a sure thing.

We cannot not bet—our very living is betting one way or the other. So says Pascal, and it becomes obvious to us all that he is right. We might base our bet on inadequate information, or we might choose to bet for less happiness or more misery—someone might decide that believing in God is more distasteful than any amount of misery. Do they really believe this? are they idiots? Nah, they must not have all the data. Yet.

---

[4] Two or three people play. On the count of three, they simultaneously put out their choice (paper, rock, or scissors) visible to all. Scissors cut paper, paper covers rock, and rock smashes scissors. Penalty for the loss is an immediate smack on the arm. A player with a losing streak can end with a sore arm. It is particularly appealing to nine-year-old boys, who smack one another with great gusto.

So we shouldn't fool ourselves that we already have adequate information to make that choice. The neat thing about this game is that peeking is allowed. The rules of the game state that each player is not only allowed to look at the other players' hands, but is actually penalized for not doing so. Eternity is a long time to be miserable.

And so to the playing out of these scenarios.

2.
You Bet!

Is it heads you win, tails I lose? Nah!
Even zero-sum is outmoded.
This game is rigged so that we would all win, if we wanted to.

What are you betting on, right this minute? Did you leave your rain gear home today, betting that the weather would be fine? Did you go ahead and ride the bus as usual, betting that it will not be struck by a terrorist bomb? Are you betting that your house will not be hit by a tornado today and blown to smithereens, so you left your most prized possessions there instead of bringing them with you? Are you betting that the earth won't be hit today by a major meteorite, so you have made plans for tomorrow and next week?

Life is a constant course of betting: Which line will be speedier at the super market? Which lane will get through faster in a traffic jam? What to study in college? Whether to take a job now, or go to graduate school? Law school? Med school? Whom to date? Whom to marry? No matter how we slice it, we are surrounded by the possibility of seemingly chance events, and our choices about how to bet on them shape our lives.

Frenchman Blaise Pascal (1623-1662) was one of the earliest scholars to make a systematic study of chance and choice. He was brilliant in mathematics, physics, etc., and his work in probability theory laid the groundwork for the subsequent development of that area of mathematics. He also published mathematical works on conic sections and cycloids, and his physics experiments on the vacuum and atmospheric pressure were ground-breaking. He designed and built an early successful calculating machine, and instituted a prototype public transportation system. His friends, correspondents and admirers included French mathematicians Fermat and Descartes, the English architect Christopher Wren, the notable royal intellect Queen Christina of Sweden, his fellow Catholics Cardinal de Retz and Madame de Sévigné, and even the indomitable atheist Voltaire.

Pascal's work in probability theory informs what may be his most popularly known piece of writing, the *Wager.*[v] It was found after his death among his papers, which were then published as *Pensées (Thoughts)*. What follows is a paraphrased and revised expansion of *Pascal's Wager.*

> ➢ *Either the Triune God exists or not.*

Hey! Wait a minute! This is a misquotation of Pascal. He doesn't say 'Triune God' – he just says 'God'.

So he does. But nevertheless there are at least three good reasons to specify the Three-Person God of Christianity—Father, Son, and Holy Spirit—rather than simply 'God'.

The first reason is literary: Pascal's treatment implies the Triune God, and it would be unfair to him not to be explicit here—remember above, he said "…the God and Father of our Lord Jesus Christ."

The second reason is biblical: the Bible's God is the Deity that enters the space/time continuum (otherwise known as human history) time after time to interact with his creation. He is the historical God of our past, present and future. The Three-Person God is implied several times in the pre-Christian Scriptures, although it is not until the early centuries of Christianity that Trinitarian theology is worked out. The Triune God came to Abraham, for example, in the form of three men, and told him that Sarah was going to have a baby:

> Then the LORD appeared to Abraham by the oaks of Mamre . . . Abraham raised his eyes and saw three men standing there. . . . He invited them to stay and eat, and told Sarah to cook bread. Then they said to him, "Where is your wife Sarah?" "Here in the tent." And He said, "I will come back next year about this time, and your wife Sarah shall have a son." Sarah was past menopause, and she laughed. And the LORD said to Abraham, "Why did Sarah laugh? . . . Is anything too hard for the LORD?" Then the men rose from there and looked toward Sodom. [Gen. 18:1-15, paraphrased and condensed]

The third reason is theological. The Trinitarian God is unique in the panoply of gods of the religions of mankind: one God, undivided, yet composed of three persons. The First Person of this trio is God the Father, the Creator of all that is. The three Persons are co-equal and co-eternal, and all three participate in the ongoing act of creation. Nevertheless, the Father is the one from whom the others proceed. The Second Person is God the Son, co-eternal with the Father, begotten of the

Father before all worlds. Hence 'begetting' describes a relationship, not an event in time. God the Son entered human history during the reign of Augustus Caesar in a remote corner of the Roman Empire, as a human baby named Jesus, born into a humble Jewish family. The Third Person of the Triune God is the Holy Spirit, co-equal and co-eternal with the other two Persons. The Holy Spirit enters human history by indwelling people who believe that Jesus is the Second Person of the Trinity. He empowers those he indwells to participate in the work of building the Kingdom of God in human society. Together, they are one God, in three Persons.

So that's the God Pascal challenges us to bet either for or against. He and I suggest *for*. We admit that we are trying to influence your vote. But only for your own good, of course. There is no dishonor in that unless Pascal and I are wrong. So read on.

How does one bet, or wager on this God? We bet by having saving faith, or belief, that God is Creator and Preserver of all that was, is, and will be, and that Jesus Christ is God who was born as man, who came into human history to save people from the power of sin. Saving faith is a gift from God that gives its recipients great joy. The Holy Spirit is the one who helps us cash it in.

The word 'joy' here has a particular meaning. In other contexts it sometimes refers to some sort of mystical ecstasy, or the sort of exuberant happiness that is associated with an especially raucous party. Here it is neither of those, although sometimes both of those go with it.

Joy, as the term is used here, is to happiness as mature married love is to the first flush of romantic love. When we fall in love there is an adrenalin rush every time we think of the object of our attention. After we have been married for fifty years, that rush is mostly a fond memory: day to day life wouldn't sustain itself very well on that in-love rush of adrenalin. We still want to please our beloved, and after fifty years we have learned how to, and how not to (which doesn't mean that we always act accordingly, since we are sinful creatures). We have gone through trials with our beloved, experienced disasters and triumphs together, built a marriage and a family, and softened one another's edges and corners. We are in it for the long haul.

With Christian joy we may or may not have a similar period of falling in love with Jesus. Many do. When I came to belief, I read Christian literature voraciously, and made myself a nuisance to some of my church friends because I wanted to talk about God or 'the Lord' constantly. (It was years later that I talked about 'Jesus'. After all, I was an Episcopalian.) "I thought as a child, I spake as a child; but when I became a man I put away childish things." (1 Cor. 13:11) The maturity of Christian joy doesn't lose the happiness of being with Jesus any more than married love loses the happiness of being with our beloved. But settling into Christian joy is even better than settling into the maturity of a good marriage: Love is good. Joy is even better.

Joy is a good feeling, but it is not merely a good feeling. This is hard to explain because I don't want to put down marital love, but a good marriage, just like any other good thing in life, is even better when it includes the Joy of Christ. Joy is steadfast, it upholds us through thick and thin, it gives us peace and strength. Marriage doesn't always do that—even a good marriage has patches of strife, anger, disappointment or mistrust.

Joy helps us to get through the bad patches of whatever is our lot in life. When we are discouraged, or had a mind-numbing set-back, when we just can't see our way through a bad situation, joy is still there like a heartbeat, supporting us, our four-wheel drive plowing us through the mud and sand of our life. Joy is part of our armor, part of our means of transport, it contributes to our nourishment. It is steady, like the drumbeat of a trireme Roman galley synchronizing three ranks of oarsmen—steady as she goes. Or like the ground bass of a chaconne, steady-freddie, running dependably underneath all sorts of glorious and inglorious tunes and harmonies and discordant suspensions. Joy (breath). Joy (breath). Joy (breath). Steady as she goes.

As we mature in our faith, the joy becomes more powerful, and even more steady. It motivates us to persist in whatever the Lord gives us to do. It encourages us to do things we wouldn't otherwise be able to do, with people we wouldn't otherwise dream of knowing—sometimes powerful people, sometimes people whom in our prideful selves we would overlook. And we share joy with one another all our lives. Joy motivates us to buy into the faith that gives us a ticket to ride. We buy the cruise, and get the gourmet meals, the mints on the pillow, and whatever else the cruise includes.

We pray, "Grant that we may love that which Thou ordaineth." Joy is the answer to that prayer. This joy is in loving what God loves. Let me repeat that:

Joy is in loving what God loves.

In order to buy into Jesus' saving us from the power of sin— in church-talk it's called 'salvation', or 'saving faith'—we must do three things:

- We must believe that Jesus is God-the-Son.
- We must be baptized—putting our action where our mouth is.
- We must testify publicly to our faith—putting our mouth where our action is..

All three are joyful things to do, theoretically, but daunting to contemplate. Even though saving faith is a gift from God, we must respond with these three actions, which are necessary to receive our saving faith, in order for faith to work in our lives. It's a coming-out-of-the-closet thing.

This gift can be useless if we don't do these outward things, so that we are refusing the gift. It is like a teenager not bothering to cash a check his grandfather sends him for his birthday. He believes his grandfather exists, but he is so jaded with worldly goods that he doesn't accept his grandfather's gift. Having a saving faith is betting, or wagering, that God exists, by putting our money and our action where our faith is.

'Betting on God' here does not mean standing up and talking before a crowd. It means changing our lives in a way that is in keeping with our faith. But we don't do it: It is something that God does in us.

The *Acts of the Apostles* tells how the first converts to Christianity bet:

> They were devoting themselves to the apostles' teaching, to the fellowship, to the breaking of bread, and to prayers. (Acts 2:42)

That's how it's supposed to be. For us today, of course our version of 'the apostles' teaching' has been written down as Holy Scriptures, so that part is studying the Bible, both individually and with others. Having 'fellowship' with other believers suddenly becomes natural and fun. 'The breaking of bread' here refers to worship together—going to church—that includes not only teaching and praise, but also Holy Communion, the meal of bread and wine that is so full of meanings that we cannot try to fathom it here. And 'prayer', talking with God, mainlines our faith.

So we shouldn't get thrown off base because we want to reject some unattractive fake Christianity. We are probably right on target in rejecting it. But we shouldn't wager by rejecting real Christianity just because we got snookered into thinking some supercilious jackanapes was a Christian, and was what a Christian is. We never can know. It is beyond our human pay grade to know whether any particular person is a real or fake Christian: we don't know what kind of belief is in his heart that makes him as he appears. Any jackanapes might be just a particularly horrible example of a worse-unto-horrible person who has been made somewhat less bad by his saving faith in Jesus.

Or not. He may indeed be a fake Christian, and not even know it himself. He may sincerely think that he is what Christianity is all about, even while being arrogant and rude.

But although we can never accurately discern which are real and fake Christians, we can and must learn to tell the difference between real and fake Christianity. (More on this in Isaiah's Log, Ch. 12) And when we find the real thing, we should bet all we have on it! This is no frivolous issue. Does the real God really exist? How should we bet?

Many people would say, "Well, that's one thing I don't need to worry about. I'm an agnostic (or, I'm an atheist) so I just don't bet at all." But they're wrong. We don't have that option, for several reasons. The first reason is a hurricane that is headed our way.

Agnostics say to themselves, "I'll just be honest about it: I don't know whether there is a God or not. I can't decide, and that's a perfectly legitimate position to take. I can honestly sit on the fence, not deciding one way or the other. What's wrong with that?" Not deciding is betting that everything is okay. Uh-oh! In many situations, ignorance is not bliss and 'tis folly to be uninformed.

Several years ago, there was a family from up north vacationing on the Florida panhandle coast.[5] The father and little girl were out playing in the gulf on a plastic swim raft. The family must not have watched the television, or listened to the radio, and didn't know that

---

[5] It is an ironic irrelevance that they were vacationing at Cape San Blas, named for the saint for whom Blaise Pascal was also named.

there was a hurricane in the Gulf of Mexico. Or if they knew about it, they had no experience that warned them of its risk to them. The sun was shining, the sky was blue, the water was calm, and everything looked glorious. But the storm surge elsewhere in the gulf sucked father and little daughter out to sea, and they were never seen again.

Somebody should have told the family about the storm, should have let them know of the risk they were taking. Weren't there neighbors who could have warned them? Where were the authorities? It's not good to be oblivious of risk. Perhaps somebody did try to warn them, and they just didn't believe the warning. The sky was blue, the sea was calm. What? Me worry? Are they trying to spoil my vacation? We'll just take a swim this morning before the storm comes, if there's a storm coming. Meanwhile, the storm elsewhere in the Gulf sucked in the water from off of Cape San é, and with it, the plastic raft with the father and daughter.

The same thing happens to atheists. They don't realize that they are betting on fair weather, when in reality the Mother of All Storms is headed their way. Somebody should tell them. And they should pay attention. What? Me worry? I'm an atheist. I don't bet on God.

Atheism claims to be a bet that the creator God doesn't exist—that the universe created itself. But even without that improbability, the claim of atheism is a trap: Atheists don't bet on No God At All. They unwittingly bet on some other god. They don't believe in the gods of any of the world's religions. But the religions of the world don't exhaust the panoply of gods that mankind worships. All of us have something that we worship.

An atheist might worship the material wealth that he acquires, thinking it can bring him a good and happy life. He might worship an accomplishment—fame, genius, political power, altruistic service to mankind—that he thinks would bring him supreme happiness. He might worship a political state of affairs, such as a world government, or universal financial equality, or some version of racial superiority, to usher in a golden age of life on the planet.

He might worship himself: his power to direct his own destiny, as the poet William Ernest Henley did:

> Out of the night that covers me,
> Black as the pit from pole to pole,
> I thank whatever gods may be
> For my unconquerable soul. . . .
> . . . I am the master of my fate,
> I am the captain of my soul.

"The master of my fate"? Hah! You're kidding, right? No human being is the master of his fate. Frank Sinatra sings, "I did it my way," and myriad followers aspire to do it either their own way or Sinatra's. According to C. F. Allison, they share a belief in the innate goodness and trustworthiness of mankind, saved not by repentance and forgiveness, but by knowledge.[vi]

Did Sinatra do it his way? No way! He was constantly nudged off-track by unexpected events that happen to have led him to a life of fame and fortune. He may have been delighted with the outcome. Or not. But he did *not* do it his way.

A man's heart plans his ways, but the Lord directs his steps. (*Proverbs* 16:9) Or as the old Jewish saying goes, "Man plans; God laughs."

Lord, we believe. Help thou our unbelief.

3.
Beautiful Dreamers, Wake Unto Me

The heart's temptation
to escape the ambiguities and problems of life
and to establish its own self as center
always contributes to a distortion of the truth.
The heart itself must bow in continual worship before God
. . . to be saved from its escape into death and from
its prison of self-centeredness.
                                    C. FitzSimons Allison [iii]

We are prone to worship ourselves: our own wants and desires, our sense that we can direct our own paths through life.

Yet we all meet seemingly chance events nearly every day that nudge our life off course. Oops! I left my wallet at home, had to go back for it, and missed my bus, making me late for an interview that might have set me on the path for a totally different career. Or: I checked out the wrong book from the library, read the one I checked out, loved it, and it changed my life. Or: I got into a conversation with somebody, went to a movie he recommended, and it made me aware of Rwandan refugees, which set me on a track that led me to working with African AIDS orphans. Who knew?

Some people are hedonists who worship themselves in the form of pleasure. But it is easy to see that a life of hedonistic dissipation leads ultimately to sorrow. My friend Joe, for example (not his name—both Joe and

Bitsy are exaggerated caricatures of people we all know), is a delightful person—suave, witty, fun—but underneath thoughtless of anyone but himself. Joe worships a modern version of Homer's Lotus Eaters: the hedonistic ideal that is to achieve the most possible pleasure in life. Some people try to die with the most toys. Joe interprets it as "eat, drink and be merry, for tomorrow we may die." He fails to take the broader view of the classical Greek Hedonists, who recognized that dissipation leads away from pleasure, not toward it. Instead, Joe spends his money and time on things that are of fleeting worth—expensive cigars, expensive whiskey, expensive women, recreational drugs, fast cars and superficial friendships.

Joe looked sixty when he was in his forties, and will probably die with unmentionable diseases and a used-up liver. He may spend his last few years surrounded by those who loathe him for the pain he inflicts. But Joe becomes more and more insensitive to others. His only sorrow seems to be his own physical pain and his emotional self-pity. He eats, drinks, and is merry—sort of merry, anyway. But he may wait a while to die. One of Joe's embodiments is *New York Times* food columnist Craig Claiborne:

> The author's comment: "The gay life, tra-la." Despite alcoholism and the ravages of elegance, Claiborne lived—unhappily, at the end—till the age of 79.[viii]

Another hedonist friend I'll call Bitsy. She started, maybe before she was a teenager, worshiping the things that money can buy—and the process of buying them. She has always looked for satisfaction from shopping for clothes, going gangbusters through her daddy's paycheck. Her greatest concern seems to be making space enough for all her shoes. She marries one husband after another, each one richer, shallower, and uglier than the last. Why men are attracted to her is a mystery. She is lavishly but sporadically generous to servants, and to people whom she is cultivating, and she is a hoot to have lunch with, if you happen to be in her graces that day. Her life is a billboard. She cultivates moneyed acquaintances, and drops any friends who can't keep up with her compulsive spending. She majors in flashy jewelry and cars. When her money gives out, she will probably stiff-arm the tradesmen who have extended her credit, and live ungratefully on the largesse of frugal relatives.

Neither Joe nor Bitsy believes in Pascal's Triune God, and neither one darkens the door of a church. I said they are caricatures, but they are not unique in this respect.

Nevertheless, not all unbelievers lead such lives. Many of my unchurched friends are as appalled at the life styles of Joe and Bitsy as I am. My friends' houses are tasteful, gracious, and not ostentatious. They read lots of books, and they like the same classical music and fine art that I enjoy. They take care of their bodies, eating judiciously but well, and get plenty of exercise. On Sundays when I am at church, the gyms, tennis courts, and golf courses are busy, full of unbelievers.

Many of these people—I'll call them Beautiful Unbelievers, or Beautiful Dreamers—give of their time and money to charities such as NPR and the SPCA, the symphony and the art museum. I too support many of these same charities. These people are usually cordial and fun. They just don't see any point in wasting time on church, and cannot understand how in the world otherwise intelligent people like some of my other friends could possibly believe all that God-stuff.

I have thought that way myself, so I can identify with their suspicions. Actually, one of the first things I did after coming to belief in God was to take an IQ test. I had always assumed that anyone who believed that God-stuff had to be somehow mentally deficient. For years I kept a Mensa[6] book prominently displayed to reassure friends that my marbles were not in short supply. I took it off display when I learned that making a high score on IQ tests does not guarantee that you're not an idiot. All this by way of saying that I, too, have been an essentially unchurched Dreamer.

These unchurched Beautiful Dreamers do believe in a god, of course—either one of their own devising, or a concept they read about somewhere. Sometimes they believe in the God of Christianity, in a rather offhand way. Alternatively, their god is perhaps some philosophy of life, such as the underlying goodness of mankind: the notion that if people weren't handicapped by poverty, dysfunctional parents, or bad laws, everyone would be good, not steal from each other, and we would all just get along. Or the idea that "history is a story of continuing human advance", which economist

---

[6] An organization for people who could score into the top one percentile (later, two percentile) on an IQ test.

John Gray points out is for some people an article of faith.[ix]

If they have such an innocent and harmless substitute for God, why might my nice, civilized but unchurched friends gain any benefit from betting that God exists? Why should they bet everything they have on him? This is the question we address here.

> *What is the probability that the Triune God exists?*

Or to put it in a more practical vein,

> *Which way should we bet?*

But why bet at all? Couldn't we just ignore the matter altogether? Ah, but we already do bet! The way we live our lives is betting one way or another. Ignoring the matter is betting on an illusion—that God does not exist. But that's not all. By not betting we're missing out on something. Here is a wee cautionary tale:

A little old lady decided to treat herself to a cruise vacation. She carefully packed not only the clothes she thought she would need, but also a supply of snack foods that didn't need cooking, because she prided herself on getting the most for her money. She reveled in the daily excursions from the ship, and made friends with several of the other passengers. The last night of the cruise she decided to treat herself to a shipboard restaurant meal, "just this once." So she dressed for dinner, and went to the dining room. Her table-mates had been wondering why they hadn't seen her before.

At the end of the meal, she asked the waiter for her check. "Oh, Madame, there is nothing to pay. All meals are included in the price of your ticket." The blood drained from her face as she realized that for more than a week she had been subsisting on peanut-butter crackers and dried fruit in her cabin while all her shipmates were dining on the finest of gourmet fare—and that she had paid the price of this wonderful food when she bought her ticket, but in her compulsive thrift, she had deprived herself of enjoying it.

Life is a cruise. We are all born with a ticket to ride, and our tickets include all the perquisites. Some people stay in their cabins eating peanut-butter crackers and raisins, not realizing that they are missing out on the real joy of the cruise! The life that God created us for includes the lobster bisque and filet mignon béarnaise of the journey. Some people unknowingly subsist on packages of cheese crackers. Poor Joe, Bitsy, and my Beautiful Dreamers.

Hannah Pylväinen, writing recently in the *Wall Street Journal*, says about her young adulthood,

> In leaving the church when I was in college, I soon saw I had not stepped into anything else. My admittance into a dubious form of atheism merited no special membership. Atheism seemed, if anything, a community that eschewed community, that strove to preserve the strength of the individual. Thus I clung to anything that might provide stability—a boyfriend, school friends, professors. But these relationships, good as some were, were largely transient—

friendships that swelled and faded in response
to the changing mileage between us.[x]

Beautiful Dreamers don't have any idea that they are
subsisting on these snack-package pleasures of life.

Matthew Arnold expresses it poetically:

> Ah, love, let us be true to one another!
> For the world,
> which seems to lie before us like a land of dreams,
> So various, so beautiful, so new,
> Hath really neither joy, nor love, nor light,
> Nor certitude, nor peace, nor help for pain;
> And we are here as on a darkling plain
> Swept with confused alarms of struggle and flight,
> Where ignorant armies clash by night.

"Dover Beach"
Matthew Arnold (1822-1888)

Poor Matthew Arnold: not even one of Homer's lotus-
eaters, but a consumer of the cheese crackers and dried
cranberries of life's cruise. Little did he realize that the
world made by God the Creator is indeed truly
beautiful, new every morning, and is chock full of joy,
love, light, certitude, peace, and help for pain. But, as
we shall see, these are the bounties of betting on God.
Bet wrongly, and we join the ignorant armies on the
darkling plain: swept with confused alarms of struggle
and flight, and the pest-attracting crumbs of peanut-
butter crackers.

Lord, we believe. Help thou our unbelief.

4.
Why Bet?

. . . the tsunami of wishful thinking that
washed across the West [taught] that you can have
sex without the responsibility of marriage,
children without the responsibility of parenthood,
social order without the responsibility of citizenship,
liberty without the responsibility of morality, and
self-esteem without the responsibility of earned achievement.
Lord Sacks, Chief Rabbi of Britain [xi]

Are these problems social? Yes, of course. But they are primarily spiritual. Of course it would be logical and advantageous for Joe or Bitsy to bet on God—they need all the help they can get, from whatever source, to avoid their errors of wishful thinking. As Lord Sacks says, though, our society's denial of the existence of the Judeo-Christian God destroys the sense of responsibility that is the glue of our social world. But our Beautiful Dreamers' appetites and responsibilities seem to be under control. They don't commit these social irresponsibilities that Lord Sacks tells us are so harmful to society. Why should they need the Judeo-Christian God?

Because the world often seems to lie before them with neither joy, nor love, nor light, nor certitude, nor peace, nor help for pain. Like the poet Matthew Arnold, most Beautiful Dreamers have heart problems that your run-of-the-mill cardiologist cannot address. They are restless for something—but what? They run away from the answer, classically given by Augustine of Hippo

(354-430). Recalling his years of fleeing to philosophies and many of the social ills that Lord Sacks deplores--anything but God—Augustine finally concluded, "Our hearts are restless until they find their rest in Thee." Allison notes that people in a secular age are ravenously hungry for that which gives them meaning, identity, and direction.[xii] They are caught in Lord Sacks's tsunami of unbelief, of wagering against God. They must bet, and do: by avoiding God. And by avoiding him, they think they are not betting. But they are mistaken. they are in fact betting against God.

We can refuse to participate in the office football pool, or on a horse race, or on a hand of penny-ante poker. We need not waste our money on lottery tickets, or at casinos. Nor risk our lives on Russian roulette, nor those potentially poisonous fugu fish that some Japanese men pay so much for.

But there are some bets we cannot refuse. If we live in hurricane territory, we bet for or against the probability that one will come our way. We may fit our windows with storm shutters, lay in provisions in case the hurricane hits us, and then not be hit. Or we may be blasé, and bet that they will all miss us. Or we may even become so frightened at the thought of a hurricane or a blizzard that we move to California, where we risk destruction by mudslides, forest fires, earthquakes, and tsunamis, and economic destruction by government bankruptcy. But we must, and do, wager.

―――

1.We bet that the hurricane will not come, and it doesn't come	2.We bet that the hurricane will not come, and it comes.
3.We bet that the hurricane will come, and it comes.	4.We bet that the hurricane will come, and it doesn't

1. By betting against the hurricane's coming, we spend no time or money getting ready for it, even though we are in the potential cone of destruction. Hence if it doesn't come, we gain both the time and money we would otherwise have spent preparing for a danger that doesn't come. But we lose any apprehension we had about not preparing. We become complacent and less likely to prepare for the next one, also.

2. If we bet against the hurricane's coming, and it comes, we stand to lose big-time! We still have spent no money on generator, plywood, candles, emergency rations, and such. But any gain there is overwhelmed by our losses. We may lose our lives. We certainly lose property. If we survive, we have no food or water stored safely. After a day or so without electricity our fridge looks like a science experiment, and we depend for food and water on the kindness of those who prepared. What was cheap before, such as potable water, is now dear. We were penny wise and pound foolish, as the saying goes. Our loss may be everything we owned: all ruined by storm surge and wind.

3. We spend time and money laying in supplies, and getting out of harm's way. If we prepare for the storm and it comes, we are devastated by the storm, but thankful that we have prepared. We have spent money

on plywood, but our windows stood firm, so the storm did us little damage. We are sad to see the circumstances of those who failed to prepare, and we reduce our own comfort by sharing with them our food and water. We need to pray for deliverance from our *schadenfreude*—our surreptitious glee in the comparative uncomfortable circumstances of others. Complacency about the pride in our own virtue, and pleasure in the failures of others, will condemn us. The battle is within ourselves.

4. If we spend money and time laying in supplies and the hurricane veers off elsewhere, we are sometimes even a wee bit disappointed that it failed to materialize. We experience pain at our loss of *schadenfreude* that is even perhaps more of a spiritual problem for us than when we are called on to share our limited supplies. Every first aid trainee wants nothing so much as a nearby heart attack or choking victim to display his heroism.

Life is not simple. It is full of situations in which the very living of it is betting one way or another. The great Swiss theologian Emil Brunner warned us that "You can avoid making up your mind, but not your life." We can self-insure against some things—the loss of things we could do without anyway, such as a vacation trip. But we cannot self-insure against a disastrous loss, such as the family wage earner's death, when mortgage payments and the children's education are at stake. And we cannot self-insure against God.

Sometimes we seek pleasure in challenges that involve a certain level of risk. For example, backpacking in the wilderness can be asking for risk. I was backpacking with our daughter Martha and our dog Heidi on the remote Susquehannock Trail in Pennsylvania when Heidi encountered the business end of a rattlesnake. It was an exciting adventure: Heidi made a complete recovery, but getting her to a veterinarian to make that happen was more adventuresome than we had bargained for. If Martha or I had been bitten, the consequences might have been far worse. But not backpacking at all because we might have an accident is an attitude I don't choose.

Life also has some risks that are unavoidable and uninsurable, such as extinction of the human race by the million-year comet. We prepare for the comet exactly the same way we prepare for the most absolutely certain event of our life: our death. After all, we're all going to die eventually, so there is no risk involved in that. No need to bet. It's a certainty. And then there are uncalculated risks—another thing entirely. They are either a result of stupidity, they are unavoidable and so incalculable, or they are a conscious or unconscious denial of the risk. "So sorry! I didn't mean to run out of gas and make you miss your plane!"

A hurricane is coming—Florida does these things. This is not the same storm that snatched the father and daughter from Cape San Blas. In another family, another hurricane, young adult brothers Hank and Buddy and their friends Larry and Lambert, prepare for it by planning a hurricane party. They lay in beer and munchies, ready to thumb their noses at the storm. Hank and Buddy's mother, Evelyn, is worried. She has seen more storms than they have, and she urges them to get off the barrier island and come to safety. But they are adamant that there is no real danger. They think it will be fun to experience the fury of the storm up close and personal. After all, the cottage has been there for seventy years—which seems like eternity to a twenty-year-old. They will be fine, they tell her, only to be swept out to sea by the storm surge, and never heard from again.

What could she have done to persuade her sons to get off the island before the storm comes? "No, son, don't do that! You boys and your friends close up the cottage and come to town! Have your party here in front of the TV!"

Persuading friends and loved ones of the danger of a situation whose danger they don't perceive is often the trickiest part of the preparation, and we sometimes fail. They just aren't convinced that the danger is real. The check she gets from the insurance company for the loss of her cottage only pours salt into the wound of losing her sons, a loss no amount of money can compensate.

During the early 1930s, Jake Goldman had a business that took him all over Europe with easy access to official papers, and he was able to help many of his friends and relatives to leave Germany and Austria early enough to avoid the Holocaust. But he failed to persuade his favorite uncle and aunt, Jakov and Leah, to leave. During his childhood and youth Jake had enjoyed visiting their house. Not only did they have an unmatched private library, and a wonderful collection of French and Viennese paintings, but also a magnificent Bechstein piano on which Aunt Leah played, with violinist and cellist friends, all of Jake's favorite Beethoven piano trios. The conversation around their dinner table was lively, something Jake missed with his more prosaic business associates.

Jake spent many hours trying to persuade them that the Nazis were dangerous, and that they should leave while they could. Uncle Jakov was not convinced of the danger. He had an important business, and had contacts and friends in high places. Unable to take their things— especially the paintings—they refused to leave. Uncle Jakov came to think Jake was being a meddling pest, and finally refused to see him at all.

Needless to say, Jakov and Leah were among those who did not survive the war. Jake was overwhelmed with grief, and burdened with guilt. Was there anything further he could have done or said to persuade them to leave? Uncle Jacov simply refused to believe in the Holocaust, even as it was happening. But believing or not doesn't make it so.

We must, and do, also bet on whether God exists, and if so, what the consequences are of our bets. Maurice Sendak, who wrote and illustrated prize-winning children's books, is quoted as saying, "I don't believe in heaven or hell or any of those things." [xiii] Hank and Buddy didn't believe that the storm would damage their house. Uncle Jakov didn't believe that his financial power and business connections could not save him from any undue inconvenience the Nazis might attempt. (Wouldn't it be wonderful if not believing in taxes, or illness, would make them go away?) But what Sendak or any of the rest of us believes has no effect on the actuality of some things. We and Sendak are dealing here with cosmic reality—weather, gravity, the forces of good and evil—and we are either right or wrong, but anyone's belief about it is irrelevant to whether we are right or wrong.

Readers have probably discerned that underlying this discussion is the ultimate issue. Christians would like to persuade friends to share the joy of their faith, and to warn them of the potential dangers they face by not sharing this joy. Christians are not looking to accumulate points for converts. They are mothers and nephews and friends concerned about loved ones. "What more could I have done to persuade them?"

In this particular game, there is no neutral position. There are no bystanders. We can't sit this one out. If we are alive, we are already playing the game. Under that protocol, it is good to be aware that we are playing, and even better to be aware of the rules. Given the evidence, apparently the only way to score is with saving faith. Christians have great concern for friends who have not yet experienced saving faith: No faith, no score.

Lord, we believe. Help thou our unbelief.

5.
Recalculating Route

Joyful, joyful we adore Thee,
God of glory, Lord of love,
Hearts unfold like flowers before Thee,
Praising Thee, their sun above.
Henry VanDyke [xiv] [7]

When I was an unbeliever, I didn't see myself as an unbeliever. It didn't occur to me that there was a Triune God to believe in. I thought those who apparently did believe in such a concept were harmless idiots. They had been caught up into an interesting religion that held a certain cultural fascination for me. I had been raised in a church-going family, so I knew the shtick.

But I had come to think that if God didn't exist, I was wasting my time on Christianity, however beautiful its culture. Nice music, good poetry, lovely vestments, excellent choreography. But if God didn't exist, if Christianity is all a pretty fiction, my Sunday mornings would be better spent at home in my bathrobe with a pot of good coffee and the Sunday *New York Times*.

Needless to say (since I am writing this) in time I came to think differently about the issue. I came to realize that the unbeliever who has only experienced the pot of coffee and the *Times* would evaluate the trade-off quite differently from the believer, who in many cases will have had some experience of both the *New York Times*

---

[7] This poem is usually sung to the tune of Beethoven's "Ode to Joy" in the final movement of his Ninth Symphony.

on Sunday morning, and also of Sunday mornings in church listening to a sermon, singing hymns, and taking Holy Communion with friends: grafted into the Body of Christ; adopted into God's family.

I contend that in most cases the unbeliever is probably basing his calculation on inadequate experience and information. When we come to a belief in God—a saving faith---we become a child of God by adoption. "God doesn't have any grandchildren," it is said: The saving faith of our parents cannot guarantee our own saving faith. No faith, no adoption. Most Christians who have acquired their own saving faith, even those who were brought up in the Church, have experienced doubt or unbelief as a part of their spiritual and intellectual growth.

Here is a letter I recently sent to one of our grandchildren.

> Dear David,
>
> You expressed puzzlement about my use of the phrase, "God doesn't have any grandchildren." I'm sure you are familiar with the theology behind it— it's just a low-brow way of talking about the doctrine of Justification. It says that no matter how much they take them to church, and no matter how hard they pray, Christian parents—the Children of God—cannot effect their children's salvation. They can affect it, and do, but they cannot effect it. When their children become believers, they also become Children of God—not his grandchildren.
>
> I don't know how the Westminster Confession expresses it—I have ordered a copy of the WC for

my library so I can look up such things. Anglicanism's Thirty-nine Articles, which date from about 1552 and are the WC equivalent for Anglicans, says, "We are accounted righteous before God, only for the merit of our Lord and Savior Jesus Christ by faith, and not for our own works or deservings. . . ." and "Faith is the instrumental means by which sinners receive justification."

Here is an old song we used to sing:

Oh you can't get to Heaven in a Ford V-8,
'Cause it can't get through that pearly gate. (Repeat)
Ain't a-gonna grieve my Lord no more.

Oh you can't get to Heaven in a PBY[8]
Cause the darned ol' thing won't fly that high. (Repeat) Ain't a-gonna grieve my Lord no more.

If you get there before I do
Just dig a little hole and pull me through. (Repeat)
Ain't a-gonna grieve my Lord no more.

The first two verses are true, but the last stanza can't happen. It goes against this account of Justification, because it ignores saving faith as its instrumental means. There are four aspects of saving faith:

1. Understanding of what is being offered by God in the Gospel;
2. Recognition that the Gospel promise is true;
3. Entrusting ourselves to Jesus and his saving work on the Cross;
4. Repentance: turning away from false gods and evil, and turning to Christ as Savior and Lord.

---

[8] What is that? I don't know, except for the context.

This is all supported by the Scriptures (see John Rodgers, *Essential Truths*, which I am giving your parents for Christmas). Nobody else can do this on our behalf. Faith is not a something we perform (so that no one can boast): It is a set of personal conditions that are mutually complementary.

A false teaching that crops up from time to time is the false notion that faith is not necessary to God's justifying work. It may be a misinterpretation of Efficacious Atonement. Hence some say, "When Jesus died upon the Cross for the sins of the world, all men were justified in the eyes of God." That seems to be the teaching of Karl Barth. [This from John Rodgers, Th.D. Summa from Basel, where Barth was on faculty. Rodgers continues:] "If this were true, the individual's salvation would be completed without the person's consent or knowledge. . . . A person cannot be saved simply objectively as if he or she were a stick or a statue. [I think the reason that Mormons are so into genealogy is that their doctrine says that they can pray their non-Mormon ancestors into Mormon Heaven. But for Christians, . . .] The subjectivity of the person has to be involved and saved. ... Nowhere in the Scriptures is salvation made a universal description of all persons in the world. ... The atoning work of Christ is personally relied upon by the sinner, if he or she is to be justified by God. Therefore, we are to invite sinners everywhere to repent and believe or be lost and live under the wrath of God. Saving faith is not optional to salvation." It is *sine qua non*. (Rodgers, 259-269)

What it says, essentially, is that if I get there before you do, I can't dig a little hole and pull you through. Jesus has already justified you and atoned for your sins by his work on the Cross. But I can't give you saving faith – you have to have your own. Romans 3:21-26: *The righteousness of God through faith in Jesus Christ [is] for all who believe . . . all have sinned . . . and are justified by his grace as a gift . . . to be received by faith . . .It was to show his righteousness at the present time, so that he might be just and the justifier of the one who has faith in Jesus.* It is your own condition of saving faith that 'pulls you through', not mine nor that of your parents.

So God doesn't have grandchildren: only children. But we have grandchildren. I suspect both of my grandmothers of praying for me, and I assure you that I have prayed for you and your salvation since before you were born. Moreover, you can start right now, if you haven't already, praying for the salvation of your future children and grandchildren. We here on earth have grandchildren, and children, and friends and loved ones, and our prayers avail much. Peter says, *The promise is for you and for your children and for all who are far off, everyone whom the Lord our God calls to himself.* (Acts 2:39)

With love and prayers, …

Whether or not we have had grandparents praying for our salvation, and whether or not there is any such thing as God, we ought nevertheless to bet by believing in God, simply out of selfishness. Because belief gives us a more pleasant, happy and productive life here on earth and avoids the discomfort of Hell. "Pleasant, happy and productive" doesn't give us a real reason to think that the object of our belief—God's existence—is publicly and falsifiably true, but they make the alternative more **_un_**appealing. "**_Un_**pleasant, **_un_**happy and **un**productive" gives us an incentive to avoid **un**belief.

Also, if it turns out true that the Triune God is indeed the Creator and Preserver of all that exists, from the beginning to the end of time, and we were made so that our hearts are restless until we find our rest in him, how much more important it is to believe in him. What if God does exist? What are the pros and cons of betting for or against His existence if he actually exists?

Here, as elsewhere, the issue is what the odds are of our coming out ahead of the game. Fifty-fifty? Actually, they're not. There are strong scientific reasons for suspecting that the universe did not just happen by accident. But that is for somebody else's book. And some of those books are excellent.[9] Meanwhile, there are several logical reasons for suspecting that somebody has been sneaking around creating the universe, molding it into the complex thing it is, and keeping it going all this time. And there are several quite valid reasons to suspect that the one who has done all this is that lovable geek we fondly call God. Or better yet, that awe-inspiring Power we worship with fear and trembling, whose face we cannot dare to behold, and whose name we must not take in vain. But who adopts us as his children anyway. Adopted by the King of kings. The Creator and Lord of the universe. Awesome. Literally awesome.

Lord, we believe. Help thou our unbelief.

---

[9] A list of suggested reading is in the appendix.

6.
Hedging Our Bets

Joy is not simply a fleeting feeling
or an evanescent emotion;
it is a deep-seated result of one's connection to God. . . .
Religious joy is always about a relationship.
Joy has an object, and that object is God.
Our joy is in God.

James Martin, S.J.[xv]

Sometimes we deny a risk that our friends and loved ones try their best to show us.

Hank and Buddy, Larry and Lambert think they can have a hurricane party, and do all their betting on a pair of aces or a straight flush instead of the hurricane itself. What could Hank and Buddy's mother have said or done to get her grown sons out of the path of that storm? They thought they were adults who could take care of themselves.

Or we deceive ourselves into thinking that our own influence is so powerful that it will exempt us from risk. Uncle Jakov and Aunt Leah denied the pathological anti-Semitism of the Nazis until it was too late. What could their nephew Jake have said or done to change his uncle's denial? Denying the danger is to wager that the danger is not real—that we are somehow protected from any dire consequences of our actions.

So it is with God.

> *Ignoring the question of whether or not God exists is to wager that God does not exist.*

Pascal says, "Not to study for finals is to wager that the world will end or that oneself will die."

> *To behave as if God did not exist is to wager that He does not exist.*

For without studying, the bettor will flunk the final. Without leaving Germany, Uncle Jakov and Aunt Leah will die in the gas chambers. Without leaving the island, Hank and Buddy, Larry and Lambert will go out to sea in their own disintegrating beach house, holding onto their poker table and watching empty beer cans float away. And without believing in God any of us may spend eternity very uncomfortably.

Let us begin this part of the discussion by acknowledging the possibility that God may not exist. It is theoretically possible, for the sake of argument, that the universe is a result of chance and happenstance. After all, not all hurricanes hit us, and of those that do, not all are devastating. Not all wars are fought by maniacs bent on genocide, although it does seem to be the trend these days.

So for the sake of covering all the bases, let us consider the result for wagering pro or con: What if God in fact should turn out to be a figment of our collective imagination? Which set of betting behaviors is more conducive to our happiness and well-being if, as in Scenarios 3 and 4 below, he does not exist?

We are not trying to imagine a world without the providence of God. We are trying to account for the phenomena of *this* world without God as the explanation for all the things we give him credit for.

Let me emphasize: Not 'a world without God', but

This world without God as explanation.

We need to account for the fun of singing in the church choir (that one isn't hard—singing in the Community Chorus is fun, too, but somehow not as much). We need to account for the simple pleasures of the Press Club,[10] the Bible Studies, the Wednesday Night Suppers and Classes, the sermons, the hymns, the just plain being with other people who have saving faith. Even if God does not exist, these phenomena still need to be accounted for. So here we go.

---

[10] The Press Club at my church is whoever shows up on Friday mornings to put the service bulletins together. This is a big job—unlike some churches that only have an agenda of hymn numbers and maybe some Scripture references, and a title for the sermon, all on a single sheet, which needs only folding. Ours needs collating, stapling and stuffing. We have a small booklet that includes a psalm written out for the congregation to read or sing together, three Scripture lessons written out (OT, Epistle and Gospel) and service music written out with notes. As a musician, I think it is sensible to include the notes, because people who read music are the ones whose voices best support the congregational singing. We also have a couple of inserts. One is the weekly newsletter, listing the names of people who need special prayer, up-coming activities, and newcomer information. The other insert contains the words and music of any songs to be sung during communion that are not in the hymnal. These are published lovingly and carefully by the Press Club on Friday mornings, and then whoever can spare the time goes out for coffee together. Press Club is a seriously joyful activity.

God or no God, when we confess Jesus as Lord and Savior, our lives are marvelously changed for the good, even though (hypothetically) it may be a baseless confession: Jesus is not God, because in this scenario there is no God.

We still have all the joy, but we are giving credit where credit is not due. Things happen in seeming answer to prayer, but there is some other explanation than that He answers the prayer. We have weird miraculous experiences after becoming Believers, but the experiences are not generated by God. He is not part of the equation at all here, except in our mistaken imaginations. Karl Marx was right: Christianity is an opiate of the people.

Readers should be forewarned that the next several chapters are flight of fancy and partially evidence-based. Even if there were no God to explain them, the phenomena of believing in him are there for all to see—the symptoms that result from saving faith seem to be predictable, just as flu symptoms are predictable in someone infected with a flu virus

It is these symptoms to which I am an eyewitness. These symptoms have been observed for two thousand years. Christians claim that the phenomena that follow saving faith are the Lord's doing, and are marvelous in our sight. So in the hypothetical situation of God's non-existence, an alternative explanation is a flight of fancy.

If God does not exist, he of course didn't make us after all. We have no God-given joy. But hey! We do have very special and specific joy: we know this from our own experience We know the grace and peace and happy little miracles that began when we achieved what we thought was saving faith. We thought these miracles were supernatural. But if God doesn't exist, of course they were not from God after all. So what could be their source, if it isn't God?

Evolution. If God doesn't exist, the most probable solution that comes to mind is that it must be a result of an evolutionary quirk in our DNA.

We have other such quirks: For example, we have been programmed to have or not to have Parkinson's Disease. If there is no God, we are thus programed by chance. Our DNA gives us a Subthalamic Nucleus in our brain. When it goes wrong, we get the tremors and other horrors of Parkinson's Disease. Our DNA also gives us the Brodman Area 25, which sometimes gets out of whack and gives us clinical depression. Distinct areas of the brain give us other involuntary behaviors such as dystonias of various kinds. So maybe there is a specific area of the brain that gives us saving faith. Or not.

One of the miracles of modern medicine is the discovery that deep brain stimulation (DBS) can counteract the symptoms of Parkinson's Disease and clinical depression, and several other such problems. Electrical wires can be placed in our brains to stimulate the Subthalamic Nucleus and counteract the Parkinson's Disease. Or other stimulator wires in the Brodman Area 25 to counteract the clinical depression, and other wires in various places for other various dystonias.

Normally we have a sense of peace when we bet on God and figuratively lay our sins at the foot of Jesus' cross. So perhaps there is a wrinkle somewhere in our gray matter that is stimulated when we bet on God, just like there is something taking care of Brodman Area 25 if we don't have clinical depression. Maybe we should call it the 'God-man Area' (groan).

It must make us kinder to other people after making a confession of faith in Christ, and more generous than we otherwise would be. It must make us want to get together periodically, and collectively worship a figment of our collective imagination that we call God. What does it matter where it comes from? In normal people this area of the brain is apparently functioning in such a way that coming to belief that Jesus is God the Son, and all that flows logically from that premise, brings joy and miracles into their lives.

So. If it were pleasurable and beneficial, and had no harmful side effects, and we could get it by betting a certain way, we would be merely rational to bet all we have on it! Bet 'yes' on options 1 and 3—that God exists. We come to believe that Jesus is God the Son, and Voila! We get joy, and all the other virtues that come with it. This kind of joy is not only a powerful motivator, but it enhances other kinds of life situations. So we should consider the pros and cons.

1.God does exist, and we bet that he exists. Voila! Joy!	2.God does exist, and we bet that he does not exist. Oops!
3.God does not exist, and we bet that he exists. Voila! Joy!	4.God does not exist, and we bet that he does not exist. Oops!

What is the calculus for Scenarios 2 and 4? Whether or not God exists, if **we bet that he does not exist**, we miss out on all that happiness, which is either a gift from God or a genetically coded set of pleasure capabilities. Presumably, missing it is comparable to missing out on the pleasures of sex, good art, and great music.

On the other hand, if we have the innate capacity of scenario 3 (or the gift from God in scenario 1), we can acquire saving faith and with it the joy. If we don't have that inborn capacity, it is perhaps like being tone deaf. An innate part of our brain that would give us great joy goes unstimulated.

We have a granddaughter who is very musical—she is now in college on a piano scholarship. Years ago she also began studying violin, and as a child she was good enough to audition into a youth symphony. A year or so later she took a battery of tests to identify her various innate capacities, and discovered that her pitch discrimination was merely average or slightly above, but not the superior capacity needed to play a stringed instrument at a competitive level. So she has concentrated on piano, an instrument where extraordinary pitch discrimination is of little concern.

I suggest that just as we all have different levels of inborn pitch discrimination, perhaps if God doesn't exist some people have a greater inborn capacity than others for saving faith. If this is the correct analysis, then people who bet against God perhaps have a sort of saving faith dystonia. After all, brains differ in their inborn configuration. But there may be a potential cure for this dysfunction. (Here goes a flight of fancy.)

If God doesn't exist, these people need not subsist on the peanut butter crackers of life's cruise. If they chose to do so, it is conceivable that they could have deep brain stimulator wires implanted, and could come to saving faith by DBS. Even in the absence of God, perhaps the belief-experience of Christianity stimulates some sort of pleasure center in the brain: something comparable to the pleasure-stimulated brains of monkeys, except on a higher evolutionary order. On that assumption, apparently coming to saving faith in Christ stimulates a specialized joy center in our brains that changes our outlook and our behavior. Jesus calls it the Kingdom of God. The *Wall Street Journal* says that neurologists don't know exactly how DBS improves brain function. But there is growing recognition that the brain operates via complex electrical circuits that sometimes malfunction, and that electrical stimulation can interrupt the errant signals. [xvi]

There are, presumably, some people who would choose not to have that part of their brain stimulated. They fight against coming to belief. I myself fought against belief. I read and re-read Francis Thompson's poem "The Hound of Heaven" and fancied myself exquisitely hounded. Those who object might consider all that joy unseemly and undignified.

Some people are puritanical in their outlook on life: severe in taste, harsh on themselves and others. Their aspect is dour and uncompromising, inflexible and austere. They are prudish in their taste: all Bach and no bacchanalia, and then only prim and reserved two- and three-part inventions, played mechanically: none of Bach's rowdy passacaglias and toccatas. These people will probably choose not to have that part of their brain stimulated, thank you just the same. If they should so choose, they could affiliate with those congregations who sing only the most staid of metrical psalms in church: not those "psalms and hymns and spiritual songs" (Ephesians 5: 19) that the rowdy-type Christians enjoy bellowing out.

I know someone whose Scottish great-grandmother was reputed (by her descendants) to have been so puritanical that although she would deign to sit in a rocking chair, she thought that to actually rock would be entirely too boisterous. Perhaps any Beautiful Dreamer who declines to experience the boisterous joy of Christianity has a brain shaped in a similar mold.

But that's okay.

Christians, complete with saving faith, come in all sorts of construction materials. Our response to God's gift of saving faith, you remember, requires that we
    Believe that Jesus is God the Son.
    Proclaim our belief publicly.
    Become baptized.

There is nothing there that says she has to rock.

It doesn't really matter whether we rock or not. Nor whether we raise our hands when we sing, or what kind of clothes we wear to church, or how we wear our hair, or whether we speak grammatically. It will follow from our belief, however, our saving faith, that we will want to put our best foot forward, whichever foot we think that is, just because we love the Lord. I know people whose idea of dressing up is to wear the T-shirt that has the most exotic Hard Rock Cafe logo on it. We want to honor the Lord the best way we know how: by speaking as grammatically as we can, dressing to honor him, training ourselves to sing well for him, and selecting the noblest kinds of music to sing and play in worshipping him.[11]

After finding the Christian belief/behavior area of our brain, it becomes the most important thing in the world to us. If we lost it we would sell everything we have to buy it back. We would die for it, and many people have in fact died for it. They've been stoned to death, beheaded, eaten by lions in the Coliseum, burned alive in their churches by jihadists who mistakenly thought they were doing their version of God a favor. Christians have gone gladly to their deaths singing hymns of praise to God, because these trials fail to destroy their real joy.

---

[11] Actually, the words matter a great deal. Whether they are sung in plainsong, or Anglican psalms, or metrical psalms, or hymns or spiritual songs, the words must be in agreement with Scripture, because music mainlines theology into the brain and heart. If we become accustomed to any music that is not in agreement with Scripture, we are in danger of wandering into heresy in our lives. Heresy is bad.

If it is that great, there is no way that most of us would
not bet on having that genetic prize!

I am apprehensive about this line of research, however,
because if its scientific basis were sound, it could
potentially be used in devious ways: It might be used
without the subject's consent, just as pre-frontal
lobotomy and forced sterilization have been used—in
this case, to bring unwilling people to belief in God, or
to circumvent a natural believer's saving faith. This kind
of power in the wrong hands could cause a repeat of
the Spanish Inquisition. On the other hand, if it brings
joy with no harmful side effects, it beats the Inquisition
hands down for simple creature comfort.

So I guess that answers part of the question about
Scenarios 2 and 4. The only way we would *not* bet that
God exists would be if we were ignorant of the
consequences of our bets, or if the neurosurgery of the
DBS procedure were so sloppy as to make its side
effects unattractive. If we were neither ignorant about
our neural anatomy, nor ignorant of the fact that the
Christian experience is one of great and undignified joy,
nor such prudes that we would prefer not to experience
that kind of joy (in which case we would refuse to rock)
then we would all be joyful.

The result of betting that God exists, given our actual
historical data providing overwhelming evidence, is joy,
love, good will toward everybody, and particularly
toward fellow Christians. We would go and sell all that
we have in order to bet on God. Even if God does not
exist, the hypothesized faith center in our brains is
worth whatever the cost.

Mind-altering drugs change our body chemistry in destructive ways, so that they make us dysfunctional. The mind-altering experiences of Christianity make us more and more functional, rather than less and less. We would become better and better at whatever we thought God wanted us to do with our lives, whether it was particle physics or pediatric nursing. We would go to church every time the church door opens, we would be in several Bible study groups, we would bring cooked dinners to the sick and to new mothers, we would run around telling all our friends and every stranger we meet how wonderful it is to have the joy. Press that bar!

The Fruit of the Holy Spirit is love, joy, peace, patience, kindness, goodness, faithfulness, gentleness, and self-control. (Galatians 5:23) Add enhanced IQ scores to those, and also the enhanced facial musculature that goes along with the love-joy-peace bit, and who wouldn't want it?!

Are we really able to do things we wouldn't have been able to do without believing in Jesus?—score higher on our GREs and LSATs, make more touchdowns, whatever? C. S. Lewis says, Yes!—that becoming believers helps us to become better than we would have been without having a saving faith. But not necessarily better than other people. If we start out grumpy, we will become less grumpy. If we start out brilliant, we will become more brilliant.

How does saving faith work in real life, without the DBS scenario? Former Florida Supreme Court Chief Justice Major Harding tells the story of how his mother explained saving faith to him when he was a little boy. They looked at the kitchen trash can, and she said, "What do you see in there?"

"Trash."

"Well, that's what we look like before God gives us the gift of Saving Faith. Do you have trash inside you? Bad thoughts about some things, such as disobedience or laziness?"

"Yes, Ma'am, I do."

"Well, that's how God sees you before you ask Jesus into your heart." Then she spread out a clean white pillowcase over the trash can.

"This is how God sees you when Jesus wipes away your sin. Does that look better?"

"Yes, Ma'm, it looks better. But the trash is still inside there."

Then she reached under the pillow case and took out a piece of trash. "That is what the Holy Spirit does. He helps you to clean up from the inside out, piece by piece, day by day."

What a brilliant mother! She both understood a rather erudite theological concept, and saw how to explain it so that a child (and we) can understand it!

Jesus' death on the cross wipes away our sin in God's reckoning. That is not to say that God the Father is being bamboozled, but to say that he credits us with Jesus' clean pillowcase payment for our sin, and reckons our sin as paid for. It's as if somebody paid our accumulation of library fines, parking tickets, bar bills, gambling debts, and topped it off with our credit card bills, student loans, and under-water mortgage. Gone! Then the Holy Spirit helps us clean up our act, one grimy bit of trash at a time.

Does this illustration apply if there is no God? Although in that case there is no atonement for sin, it still must work. As of now, anyone who comes to saving faith apparently gains several points on his or her kindness, gentleness and self-control scores and maybe on the I.Q. scores, too. If it's not the Holy Spirit, then it must be our DNA reaching into that trash can pulling out the grumpies. We are more pleasant than before, when our natural disposition was grouchy, but not necessarily more pleasant than someone with a naturally sunny disposition. There are non-believers who have both Intelligence Quotients and Patience Quotients higher than many believers, depending on their natural propensities. But the theory is that these qualities in the non-believers would be enhanced even more by their coming to saving faith. I assure you that mine were.

So it looks as if we should go for the belief-package that Pascal recommends: the prayer, the confession of faith, the baptismal water, the corporate worship, even if God does not exist, just to take advantage of the hypothesized evolutionary genetic benefits.

Or whatever particulars our faith community has that serve the same purposes: Certainly a practice of private prayer and Bible reading. Going to church and Sunday School, being part of a weekday Bible study group of some sort. Singing in the choir, taking altar flowers and Holy Communion to shut-ins. Going to church suppers and weekday study classes. Going on weekend retreats, Whatever floats your particular boat. Because the game is float or sink.

Disclosure statement: If any readers labor under the misapprehension that evolution and deep brain DNA is a serious hypothesis for the underlying cause of Christian behavior, let me assure them that this proposal is offered *lingua in gena* (tongue in cheek). This is in complete accord with the widely held reputation of Christians as cheeky in the extreme.

Lord, we believe. Help thou our unbelief.

7.

Moonless Darkness

A symphony has a climax,
a poem builds to a burst of meaning,
but we are unfinished business.
No coming together of strands.
The game is called because of darkness.

Daphne Merkin [xvii]

Beautiful Dreamer: "The game is called because of darkness!" What does she mean? What game is called because of darkness?

Pascal II: Our game, dahling! The game of life. Snuffed. Black as the Pit from pole to pole, remember? Death.

BD: She's right! Our lives are pointless like a scribble, and then are erased. Not symphonies, with a sonata allegro form first movement, and other movements that make sense, and then a climax that feels like such a glorious ending that the audience bursts into applause! But that is the composer's doing. Without a composer, we are a meaningless scribble. Our lives are all a jumble of events, and seldom have anything like a climax.

Pascal II: Ah, but if we have joy, it's because we have a composer. At least we assume that we do, because of our joy. Or we have joy because of the composer.

BD: Oh yes, that. But what if an unbeliever doesn't want to stimulate his joy button?

Pascal II: You mean, What if he is a stiff-necked stick-in-the-mud who prefers staying with his unexceptional mental experiences, his present set of unbelieving friends (instead of bringing his friends also into the joy of belief in Jesus), and so on? If he is willing to forego the enhanced genetically driven experience of Christianity, perhaps he would consciously decide to bet against the existence of God. Maybe he prefers peanut butter crackers to lobster and prime rib.

BD: If there is in fact no such thing as God, and his bet wins, then why not? If God doesn't exist, wouldn't he gain an advantage by betting against God's existence?

Pascal II: Oh dear! No, dahling, not by a long shot. Not only would he miss the earthly pleasures of love, joy, peace, *et cetera*, but ... oh, fiddlesticks! We owe our audience here full disclosure of all the consequences of such a wager, before anyone pulls the arm of that Great One-Armed Bandit in the Sky. We should tell them everything, in spite of the fact that telling them is unpleasant in the extreme. Many clergy never mention this little dark secret to their congregations, because it is so nauseating to talk about. Its very name has become a cuss-word. Its discussion is anathema in the most Progressive Christian circles. It is sometimes disparagingly called a choice of either "Pie in the sky bye and bye", or "Fire, and it's dire, when we die". I'm talking about Hell.

BD: Oh, good grief! Don't tell me you actually believe in Hell!

Pascal II: Hell? No! Not simplistic Hell, of course. It's pretty certain that even if God does exist our physical bodies do not go to Heaven or to a place of fire and brimstone. But the evolutionary experience is something that turns out to be a very creditable substitute for your classic Inferno. Jesus mentions an unpleasant after-life several times, not threatening anyone with it, but warning them against it. But even if God didn't exist, apparently, there has evolved in our species an eternal loop of Hell-like experience. It's not a place, but an infernal Dream that allows no escape. No exit (with no apologies to Sartre—it's apparently more like Doré's illustrations for Dante's Inferno than like Sartre's play). Nightmare. Never wake up. No fascinating conversation.

Hell is not specific to Western culture. It shows up in Japanese art, and other Eastern civilizations, the Near East, and historical and traditional Western culture.

But most Europeans and Americans nowadays don't believe in Hell at all. Most people think of the after-life as whatever it was in life that the dead person enjoyed most in life. That might be an eternal game of bridge, or an eternal rod and reel catching humongous fish. I recently attended a funeral where the clergyman, speaking from the pulpit, gave every indication that the dear departed probably would be already playing the eighteenth hole and heading for the clubhouse bar. I'm not making this up. Or at least not most of it.

The prevailing serious understanding of what happens to people after death is that they go into a deep and permanent sleep—as Allison puts it, a final oblivion with no accountability.[xviii] Many people who commit suicide are lulled by that assumption into killing themselves—"I will just go to sleep and escape from the problems that are troubling me here in this life." Well, dahling, they probably are in for the shock of their lives—or the shock of their deaths. Wake up and smell the sulphur!

Before the advances of modern medicine, there was no solid evidence about Hell one way or the other. Nowadays, I'm afraid, there is lots of evidence that either God or Evolution has programmed into the human brain what seems a lot like the real thing, or at least like Dante's and Milton's versions of the real thing. We get this information from people who have had Near Death Experiences (NDEs). They were clinically dead, but were resuscitated by the miracles of modern medicine. In NDEs those of us who bet for God are rewarded by a more than pleasant eternal Dream. The evidence also indicates that those who bet against God are in for an unpleasant surprise after death. Wake up and smell the sulfur!

Before the advent of medical NDEs, tradition told it this way: According to the Bible, we have a choice between Heaven and Hell. The price for the ticket to get into Heaven is simple: a saving faith. For those who have rejected the Triune God, there is an existence of sorrow, an unending loss of all good, combined with a remorseless perpetual anger awaiting us after death. Those in Hell are banished from fellowship with God and the community of saints, and dwell under God's condemnation forever. Such suffering hardens and embitters; it does not lead to repentance. But that, of course, assumes that God exists. I've no idea if repentance has any significance to the Hell loop of unbelievers if God doesn't exist.

Then there's the problem of Heaven seeming so deadly to unbelievers—all those saintly boring Christians there. "All the interesting people are in Hell, anyway. I'd much rather go to Hell, and visit with Bernard Shaw and Aldous Huxley, than go to Heaven with Mother Teresa." The problem, of course, is that Hell is not dreamy afternoons at a sidewalk café. If God does not exist, nothing changes but the theology. John Rodgers points out that the suffering in Hell is described graphically in the Bible as eternal punishment, eternal fire, a lake of fire, weeping and wailing and gnashing of teeth. There will be degrees of suffering and dishonor proportionate to the light rejected and the life lived.[xix]

So your grandmother was right if she said "God will get you for that!" Each of us gets his just deserts.[12] There is the little nonentity of a bus driver who simmered a race hatred and class warfare grudge. He took revenge on people who rode his bus by jerking them around as much as he could, and being as churlish as possible. After many years of practice, that was churlish indeed. He doesn't get the same Hellish celebrity treatment, though, as Hitler or Stalin. Their punishment is so exquisitely painful that we cannot even fathom it. And don't want to. But the bus driver's Hell is Hellish, nevertheless. Doré's illustrations for Dante's *Inferno* are graphic indeed.

---

[12] Only one 's' in 'deserts': no sweet desserts in Hell.

Many people claim that even if God does exist, there is no such thing as Hell. They say that a loving God would not consign anyone to Hell. But it is Jesus, in the very human embodiment of the love of God, who implicitly says that it is not God who consigns people to Hell after death, but they themselves by rejecting God. The Bible says a lot more about Hell than it says about Heaven. One picture Jesus draws is of the sheep and the goats:

> When the Son of Man comes in his glory, and all the holy angels, all nations will be before his judgment throne, and he will divide them, sheep to his right, goats to his left. Then he will say to the sheep, "Come, my father's blessed ones, inherit the kingdom prepared for you before the founding of the world. Because when I was hungry you fed me, etc." And they said, "When did we feed you?" "As often as you did it to the least, you did it to me."

> Then he said to the goats, "Depart from me, you cursed, into the *everlasting fire prepared for the devil and his angels.* I was hungry and you gave me no food, etc." "Lord, when did we see you hungry and not feed you?" "I tell you, if you failed the least of these, you failed me." And they will go to everlasting punishment, but the righteous to eternal life. (*Matthew* 25.31-46, abbreviated)

Jesus' teaching about Hell is not a threat but a warning, out of love and concern that no one should take the attitude that would cause him to suffer Hell.

God does not consign anyone to Hell who is begging to go to Heaven. They put themselves there. Each person gets exactly what they want. If someone wants to spend eternity with God, on God's terms, he will find himself being escorted through the Pearly Gate. If someone does not want to have anything to do with God, or at least not on God's terms, then he gets exactly what he wants, also. He gets eternal separation from God. And if he has been nasty to God's creatures, including his fellow human beings, he gets his just deserts, which will not be pleasant.

So some people knowingly plan to go to Hell, and make jokes about it: "The people in Hell are much more interesting," they say. But Hell may be somewhat different from the quaint little Hell they imagine, with all of the most fascinating people ready to welcome them. There may not be much chance for scintillating conversation over tea with Mussolini and Adolf Hitler if they have to spend all their time rolling stones uphill, and prodding each other with pitchforks and doing all manner of unpleasant things to one another.

An important distinction between Hell and the hurricane party or the holocaust is that almost nobody comes back to tell about it. No one on earth knows for certain who is there. Nobody can testify as to the results of the risk-taking. We are told that roughly fifteen percent of NDEs are hellish. But that only tells us about the people who came back and admitted to experiencing it. What about those who come back but don't tell anyone that they were about to go to Hell?

What about those who die and are not given the option of coming back to life? What percentage are they?

Evelyn, who before the hurricane had warned and pleaded with her sons, is left to live the event over and over in her mind, wishing she had been able to forcibly bring them to safety as she had when they were toddlers. Her sons and their friends no doubt had time to repent of their decision not to heed her advice, as they felt the house breaking up in the storm surge, and watched the empty beer cans float by. Jake, who warned and pleaded with his uncle, is there to flagellate himself for not being more persuasive. My student can bemoan his own risk-taking publicly, after he has failed his finals. Uncle Jakov and Aunt Leah probably bemoaned their risk taking in the cattle cars on the way to Auschwitz, and in the final hours and minutes of the horrifying results. "Jake is such a good boy. Why didn't we listen to him?"

A happy distinction between Hell and these lesser disasters is that there is no way out of the storm for the party boys, nor is there a way out of the cattle cars headed for Auschwitz. There is, however, a chance of late-in-life conversion that plucks us off the slide into Hell, if our mental and moral faculties are still working. Deathbed conversions are possible even as we approach the Pearly Gate. It is not marked "Arbeit macht frei", from which none could choose not to enter. If St. Peter, as in cartoons, is standing there like a maître d', as arbiter of seating at that Great Banquet in the Sky, we have that great crib sheet telling us what to say to get in: written on its arch, "Help me, Jesus!". Even at this penultimate step, the sinner—i.e., all of us—can choose to plead for mercy, acknowledge Jesus as the one who can save him from the jaws of Hell, and can flee to the bosom of Abraham. *Oh, rock-a my soul.*

How much more preferable it is to have a God who exists, and is merciful and gracious, and can understand and identify with a frail human being, who begs forgiveness with his final breath. How much better he than a non-existent god, substituted by a quirk in our DNA that gives us an endless dream of Hell if we fail to testify to our faith in our lifetimes. God forgives. DNA is not known to.

The souls in the Hell dream cannot give a testimony to their mistake. They can wish for all eternity that they had been less selfish and prideful, but their wish itself will be selfish, not penitent.

In the New Testament, Jesus tells it like this:

> There was a rich man who was clothed in purple and fine linen and dined sumptuously. A beggar named Lazarus, full of sores, was at his gate, hoping to eat the crumbs from the rich man's table. The beggar died, and was carried by the angels to Abraham's bosom. The rich man also died and was buried. He was in torment in Hades, and he saw Abraham far off, and Lazarus in his bosom.
>
> Then he cried, "Father Abraham, have mercy on me, and send Lazarus to dip his finger in water and cool my tongue, for I am tormented in this fire." But Abraham said, "Son, remember that in life you had good things, and Lazarus

bad, but now he is comforted and you are tormented. And besides, there is a great gulf between us and you, so that those who want to go from here to you cannot, nor can those from there come to us."

Then he said, "I beg you, father, send him to my father's house, for I have five brothers, to testify to them, so they should not also come to this place of torment." Abraham said to him, "They have Moses and the prophets;. They can hear them." And he said, "No, father Abraham, but if someone goes to them from the dead, they will repent." But he said to him, "If they do not hear Moses and the prophets, they will not be persuaded even if one rise from the dead." (*Luke* 16:19-31)

So Jesus' followers took the story to heart, went out and fed the poor in soup kitchens, and ministered to the sick and lame. "You gave no chicken soup," Lazarus lamented. And that is how hospitals first were invented.

There are two responses to this parable. One response is to go out and work for the Kingdom of God: by donating time, effort and money to meet the felt needs of the hungry, the sick, the homeless, the friendless, and the needy. And also by addressing their ultimate real need: to know and believe in the Lord Jesus Christ, and so to give them the gospel along with food and shelter.

The other response is to say, "That's just a metaphor. We are to take it to mean that Heaven and Hell are here on earth, and it is our duty to vote into public office people who use public resources to build more soup kitchens and homeless shelters. But to mention Christianity to them would be an intrusion on their privacy."

Those who say this assume that there is no such thing as Heaven or Hell after death. And if their assumption were correct, then leaving the needy to their own devices would be harmless. But Hell, or its experiential equivalent, seems to be the default position, whether God exists or not. Absent saving faith inspiring us to befriend the needy, everybody gets the Hell experience we all deserve.

Hence everybody needs to be warned so they can take measures to avoid disaster. The family on Cape San Blas who lost daughter and father to the unseen storm, Uncle Jakov and Aunt Leah who lost their lives in the gas chamber, Hank and Buddy and their friends swept out to sea with Evelyn's beach house, Joe, Bitsy, Beautiful Dreamers—all needed to be warned. But warning people of imminent disaster is often an unpleasant thing to do. The messenger often gets blamed for the message, and even worse, for making up the whole thing. But we would be remiss unto our own condemnation if we fail to warn. And sometimes, just sometimes, the warning is not an exercise in futility.

There are various ways to weasel out of believing in Hell. One is by claiming that those who don't make it into Heaven simply don't wake up at all. That claim is that Hell is empty. Others say that some people go there, but only for a period of time. After sufficient suffering they go out of existence. Jesus says otherwise, and he's the one in charge of giving out tickets to goats and sheep.

The evolutionist has a different take on the rationale, but the facts are of course the same. The data we have now, not available to prior generations, are from near death experiences (NDEs) of people who were clinically dead but were revived by the miracles of modern medicine. A percentage of them wake up remembering the experience of dying – of floating up to the ceiling and seeing the medical team working to restore life to their body, and/or of entering a tunnel with a bright light at the end, with Jesus and loved ones meeting them, and all sorts of other pleasant reasons to want to stay. Many came back to life only reluctantly. Others might have decided not to come back – we will never know about those until we ask them ourselves.

Other NDEs give the dying a taste of Hell. Those probably all come back to life, if given the option. These NDEs tell us that death does not lead to a permanent sleep and oblivion. We are all programmed so that during death we have a closed-loop experience, a dream that takes us from the penultimate neuron firing of the living brain to an ultimately permanent, eternally-seeming-to-repeat sensation of either the incense of Heaven or the sulfur of Hell, depending on whether or not we activated our saving faith during our earthly lives.

NDEs were rare until defibrillators and other life-saving devices had the unintended consequence of an entire genre of literature: first-hand accounts of dying. I suggest that readers google "near death experiences" and see what they find. It can be interpreted to imply that if God exists, Heaven is a pleasant place. Jesus is there to greet his own, as are their friends and relatives from here on earth. If there is no God, then evolution has programmed people who do not come to a saving faith in the Triune God (by betting the right way) to have a very unpleasant after-life.

Here is a brief and somewhat random sampling from the internet:

> "... according to some estimates as many as 15 percent of NDEs are Hellish" (Blackmore 2004: 362).
>
> There are numerous reports of bad NDE trips involving tortures by elves, giants, demons, etc. . . . .
>
> Moody . . . . is sure that NDEs are evidence of consciousness existing separately from the brain. He thinks that NDEs prove the existence of life after death. *Skeptics, on the other hand, believe that NDEs can be explained by neurochemistry and are the result of brain states that occur due to a dying, demented, extremely stressed, or drugged brain. For example, neural noise and retino-cortical mapping explain the common experience of passage down a tunnel from darkness into a bright light.* . . . .
>
> Blackmore attributes the feelings of extreme peacefulness of the NDE to the release of endorphins in response to the extreme stress of the situation. The buzzing or ringing sound is attributed to cerebral anoxia and consequent

effects upon the connections between brain cells (op. cit., 64).

It doesn't really matter what the scientific cause is for NDEs. We now can be nearly certain that instead of the dreamless sleep of death that so many people assume is in store for them, there is either a real Heaven and Hell, or a pre-programmed dream or hallucination in an endless loop that our minds lock into as our bodies die. If we have bet on saving faith, our programmed dream loop is Heaven, where we stand around the throne of God, casting our crowns before him and worshipping him throughout eternity.

Okay, okay, this sounds just like Hell to some people. Heaven is an acquired taste. But we are strongly motivated to acquire a taste for it when we apprehend the alternative. Consider church as choir practice for the Heavenly Choir. Life is not only a cruise, it is also a choir audition. And if we pass, we are all given beautiful voices when we check in at the Pearly Gate.

We have a glimpse of the endless loop in the final stanza of the hymn, "Amazing Grace":

When we've been there ten thousand years
Bright shining as the sun
We've no less days to sing God's praise
Than when we'd first begun.

Surely Beautiful Dreamers would not knowingly choose Hell, even if it's only an inescapable dream.

Somebody needs to warn them.

8.
Welcome Home

My song is love unknown
my Savior's love to me,
love to the loveless shown
that they may lovely be …

Samuel Crossman [xx]

One of the miraculous things about Christians is that they are always lovable—to other Christians, at the very least. Loving one another is part of the miracle of Christianity. One of the first Bible verses I learned as a toddler was, "Little children, love one another." (John 13:33-34 and I John 4:7) Jesus commands us to love one another, in spite of our foibles, and He gives us enough heavenly grace to do it. More or less. It's a miracle. That is God's job, and he does it rather well.

It says right there in plain print that Christians are sinners, just like everybody else, but with several advantages: First, we acknowledge our sinfulness. Second, we ask for and get forgiveness. And finally, we are given grace to actually become better than we would have been without the grace. As a result, Christians have more fun. It may seem paradoxical, but the claim here is that Christians have more fun both than other people (who aren't Christians), and also more fun than they would have if they weren't Christians.

Some church-goers assume that they themselves are Christians, when they are actually Rice Christians. Nineteenth and early twentieth century Christian missionaries to China fed the people who came to the mission. Hungry people flocked to the missions for their bowls of rice, and it was often assumed that among them saving faith was rare.

Then China expelled all the foreign missionaries, not to allow westerners to return until after both World War II and a long era of closed Communism. When again Christians could go to China, they found there an underground Christian Church thriving under the leadership of these former supposed Rice Christians. It turns out that many of the supposed Rice Christians were actual believers, even then, and God gave many others saving faith when push came to shove.

The term 'Rice Christian' as used here applies not only to the hungry Chinese at the missions, but also to people in the Western world who have some reason for considering themselves Christians, but don't yet have a saving faith in the Lord Jesus Christ. Feeding hungry people—whether it is feeding their animal tummy hunger, their human hunger for friendship, or their souls' hunger for God—is a way for them to learn what Christianity is all about. Rice Christians go to church and associate with Christians, because it feels like fun. And those Christians seem to be having such a good time. So they become a part of it. They don't realize that there's something they are missing. Sitting in church doesn't alone make people Christians, any more than sitting in a garage makes them cars. But the odds of metamorphosis are better for the church than for the garage. Most of us have done time as Rice Christians. But a lot of church occupants don't yet have saving faith, which includes

- Believing the package: that the Lord is our Maker and not we ourselves, and that He is one God in Three Persons.
- Loving the Lord with all our heart, and wanting to study and learn everything he gives us to know about him,
- Loving his creation: from birds and trees to unchurched neighbors, wanting to participate in bringing it into communion with him,
- Warring with the devils inside ourselves that keep us from being in full communion with him, and
- Loving other Christians and wanting to hang out with them.

Rice Christians belong to a Christian church, and have most of the trappings of Christianity. But until they have a shift of alignment in how they view their world—a *metanoia*—they miss out on most of the fun, the essence of the faith. They are eating peanut-butter crackers in their stateroom when they could be having rare roast beef and Lobster Thermidor in the dining room of the cruise ship of life.

Even other Christians can't tell the real Christians from the counterfeit ones. And the Rice Christians don't even realize that they don't have the real thing. As I said earlier, when I was an unbeliever I didn't realize there was really anything to believe.

I knew a man, Fletcher was his name, who had been an Episcopalian all his life, and was the Senior Warden of my church. When I came to belief I thought he was a model Christian. But much later he came to genuine belief and trust in the Lord. What a beautiful revelation it was when fifteen or so years later Fletcher came to real belief! His life became truly rich. He began new friendships with fellow church people, and also with un-churched friends. He became a life-line for people at various nursing homes, and he took great joy in doing it. He found the Lobster Thermidor and champagne of life, and enjoyed every bite and sip.

One of the miraculous things about Christianity is that the Lord gives his people an urge to do what he wants them to do, and gives them pleasure and joy in doing it. He also usually makes them good at doing it.

If the Lord wants one of his believers to become a medical missionary to lepers, He gives him a medical education, a fascination with leprosy, a love for lepers, and a *joy* in being with lepers (along with the rest of the package of wanting to learn more about the Lord, etc.). It's a very efficient system, which works only because of His omnipotence, not to mention His loving kindness to lepers.[13]

One of the perhaps silliest songs we sing goes like this:

> The jo-hoy of the Lo-ho-ho-hord is my strength
> The jo-hoy of the Lo-ho-ho-hord is my strength
> The jo-hoy of the Lo-ho-ho-hord is my strength
> Oh the jo-hoy of the Lo-hord is my strength.

---

[13] You might say, "Why doesn't He just do away with leprosy, if He can do all that?" That's another fascinating branch of theology.

Refrain:
Ha **ha** ha ha ha **ha** ha ha ha **ha ha ha,**
Ha **ha** ha ha ha **ha** ha ha ha **ha ha ha,**
Ha **ha** ha ha ha **ha** ha ha ha **ha ha ha,**
Oh, the Jo-hoy of the Lo-hord is my strength.

I am a classically trained musician with a master's degree in musicology. I regard it a major miracle that I enjoy singing that song. The tune won't win any awards, and although the words are from the finest poetry in Western literature, they are not set to their poetic advantage. Nevertheless, the testimony is right on target.

Grace happens. When the Lord decides it is nearing the time when an unbeliever should come to belief in him, he causes at least one Christian—sometimes several—to really like him, even if he is a first class jerk. That Christian wants to get to know him, pray for him, do things with him, make friends with him. The Christian genuinely likes him, and wants him to be saved from being swept out to sea, or into the gas chambers. He wants to be part of the process when the Lord brings that unbeliever to saving faith. It's not voyeurism, or peak bagging, or bird ticking, or any of those self-serving preoccupations. It's more like art or music appreciation—like wanting to watch a glorious December sunrise over a bay, or listen to a magnificent symphony played by a top orchestra.

But is it too late for some unbelievers? "I am too old to become a believer. I can't change my life now—this is who I am. There is no way in the world that I am going to start singing about the jo-ho-hoy of the Lo-ho-hord at my age. Besides, why would God want me at this stage of life? I can't go to med school and become a medical missionary to lepers. I would be no good at all to him." But Jesus says, "I tell you that there is more joy in Heaven over one sinner who repents than over ninety-nine virtuous people who don't need to repent." (*Luke* 15.7) And I might add that Heaven's joy trickles down to the Lord's Kingdom here on earth, so that all Christendom rejoices.

Jesus tells the story of the man who owned a vineyard. His grapes were ripe, and he needed pickers and stompers. So he went to the employment office and hired some people to come and work for him for a thousand dollars a day. Then about noon some more people came along, and asked for a job, and he sent them to work. Later, when it was nearly quitting time, some more people straggled over and asked if they could work, and he sent them in to work, too.

When quitting time came, they all lined up for their wages, and the first ones each got a thousand dollars, just like he said. (I know that's a lot of money for unskilled labor, but the Lord is gracious, plenteous in mercy, and he pays well.) The ones who had worked since noon also each got a thousand dollars. Then along came the people who had been working only an hour or so, even those who had staggered in on their very deathbeds, and he gave them each a thousand dollars, too. The ones who had been there all day objected. They said, "Lord, we have been coming to your church, laboring in your vineyard all day in the hot sun, counting your money, singing in your choir, bringing covered dishes to your potluck suppers, and you give these newcomers just as much joy as you give us. What's up? Isn't that unfair?"

And the Lord said, "What's it to you if I give the newcomers as much joy as I give you? Go on and enjoy the joy I give you. I give everybody as much joy as they can stand. If you can deal with being more joyful than you already are, go to it! It's yours!" And they all sang about the Jo-ho-hoy of the Lo-ho-hord of the vineyard, and rejoiced in their new fellow workers.

Eventually, that is, sort of. Remember? We're human. (Matthew 20, with great liberties)

This is what else Scripture says about it:

God made us. We are human. He cares about each of us because he is brilliant and can not only keep up with each of the hairs on our heads, but he can also remember our names. We each were born into the human family, God's household and creation. But sometime in our spiritual childhood, we said, "I'm going to take my dollies (or my ball and bat) and run away. I'm going to go and play where God's prying eyes can't see me." And so we went off with our toys, and grew up ignoring the Father's household.

But bye and bye our life seemed empty. We had a crisis, a series of crises—or we just gradually realized that our life was dry, pointless, rich in empty things, and poor in whatever it was we were missing. We might find ourselves humming one of those churchy tunes, like "Amazing Grace", and wondering what it would feel like to just sit at the back of a church and watch. We might, even at our stage of life, go to the Father's household . . . maybe just stay around the edge, where nobody would notice.

But what does Jesus say about our situation? He says that the Father sees us coming, ignores his dignity, picks up his skirts and runs out to meet us. He says to everybody hanging around, "Happy day! He is coming back! Let's have a party! Kill the fatted calf, chill the best champagne, let's celebrate my child's return!"

He invites the whole neighborhood in to feast in our honor. We are welcomed with open arms, fêted, included, and the angels in Heaven are flying around knocking fists and giving each other high fives.

But our brother, who was always Goody-Two-Shoes, is green-eyed with jealousy. Hey! Why does he get asked to sit on the vestry, or be an elder, or give his testimony to a group, when I've been here all along, and nobody asked me to do anything like that!"

The Father tells him to cool it—that he should have been out looking for us, to bring us home long before we decided to come back on our own. He is being unchristian, and he should have known enough from his Hebrew lessons, catechism classes, and adult Sunday School courses to realize not only that he was loved all along, but that he is his brother's keeper, and should have had our welfare in focus. He should be as delighted to have us back as God Himself was.

So the brother, too, finally gets around to joining a Bible study group and becoming a real Christian instead of the Rice Christian he was before. He might even go on an Anglican Fourth Day[14] weekend, and start high-fiving with the angels. And everybody lives happily ever after.

That is a much revised version of the Prodigal Son, which ought to be called the Loving Father, and basically it says this: Whenever we come to the Father, He welcomes us. Whatever degree of party-time we want, that's what we get. The father is joyful, and we are, too. It is a far-and-away joyful event. (Luke 15:11-31)

The neat thing about the return to the Father is that it doesn't matter when, or what the circumstances, the Father and his friends rejoice in our coming. He is not sizing us up as a worker, looking us over to see what we can do for him. He is rejoicing in our escaping the clutches of evil, even if only on our deathbed. So . . . we barely manage to crawl onto the Father's domain, and collapse there just past its frontier, drawing smooth breaths of its sweet life-giving air. We find great comfort there, peace, a sense of inner joy. And then we die. Our death rattle is "Thank you, Jesus!" It may sound like a rattle to those in the world, but to the heavenly host gathered around our earthly body waiting

---

[14] The three-day little course ("Cursillo"), an immersion weekend course in basic Christianity, given at an overnight facility. In some denominations it is called Anglican Fourth Day, in others Cursillo, Walk to Emmaus, Via de Cristo, Unidos en Cristo, Kairos, Presbyterian Pilgrims, Great Banquet, Credo Recovery, Chrysalis Community, Encounter Christ—there may be other names. It is intensely joyful.

to escort our souls, it is a triumphant clarion cry of victory. By coming to saving faith, we have conquered death—or at any rate, Jesus has done it for us. It no longer has dominion over us. "Thank you, Jesus! Amen and amen!" Death bed conversions happen all the time. Does that mean that we are worthless, because we had only hours, or minutes, or seconds, to live as a Christian, as a Believer? Au contraire! Boy, are we in for a happy surprise!

We don't have just a few minutes, we have all eternity.

It is true that if we delay belief to the last minute we miss out on a lifetime of fellowship, of joy, of Bible study, of Press Club camaraderie, of the Daughters of the Holy Cross. But the Father not only welcomes us with open arms, he is there with a host of angels, and also a host of fellow Christians—the Church Expectant—rejoicing in our salvation! No matter how late we are to our party, this is the Party of all parties, the eternal celebration. The lost child has come home. Hallelujah! For the Lord God Omnipotent reigneth!

But is there any difference in eternity if God is in charge, or if he doesn't exist? Is all flesh, all our lives, nothing but grass that is alive and green one day, and goes brown and dies the next? Is there any advantage of to us of God's existing, or not, if we bet that he exists and get the right dream loop?

Well, of course the way we bet has no influence at all over whether or not God actually does or doesn't exist. He does, or he doesn't. His existence is either factual or counter-factual. The way we bet may only influence our personal, private outcomes—of having joy in life or peanut-butter crackers, and Heaven or Hell for eternity. And our perception of Heaven (or Hell) may be no different to us, whether we are locked into an endless loop of after-life experience generated by our DNA, or whether we are actually in Heaven (or Hell) in an accidental universe.

But Heaven is infinitely better if God does exist. If God exists and we go to Heaven (or Hell) the experience is real and shared. If we meet our mothers, or Mother Teresa, or Martin Luther King, they are meeting us, too. It will not be a figment of our DNA-generated imagination. The angels in heaven are truly and objectively rejoicing for our triumph over death. Our loved ones are also rejoicing as they escort us triumphantly to the throne room of everlasting praise of the Godhead.

And Hell may be infinitely better, too. After all, the God who made Heaven and Earth is merciful and gracious, and will not punish us more than we deserve, whereas hallucinations can't be trusted to be merciful or just. The DNA Heaven and Hell are both generated by the brain itself, although we may not be able to tell the difference. Other beings in the experience are fictitious, like the population of our dreams. Whatever is experienced in the NDEs may echo a painting by Matthias Grünewald and seems to its subject like an infernal eternity, but objectively it wound occur in a fleeting moment—perhaps a blip on the screen interpreting the electrical impulses of the dying brain. Nevertheless, it seems as if it inescapably lasts forever.

There we will be spending eternity praising God in the company of all the faithful from generation unto generation. Just think! Singing in the same celestial choir with Bach, Handel, St. Ambrose, St. Gregory and St. Cecilia—and not thinking of them at all, but with every fiber of our being focused on nothing but the One our singing glorifies. That will be the Hallelujah Chorus indeed.

Lord, we believe. Help thou our unbelief.

9.
The Rest of the Story

"Lord, if this is how you treat your friends,
It's no wonder you have so many enemies."
Saint Teresa of Avila

I don't want to mislead anyone: Christianity is not all wine and roses. Jews and Christians seem to be the only groups who are acceptable as the objects of hate speech these days. Among the east and west coast intelligentsia, at Harvard and UCBerkeley we are pariahs. They think all the troubles of the world are caused because we Christians are so obnoxiously outspoken about our faith, and they seem to dislike Jews just because they always have. We analyze and find fault with the theology of other religions, and they think our analysis and critique is the cause of their bombings and killings. The otherwise civilized ones discriminate against us brazenly. They make fun of us.

Hey! We make fun of ourselves. There must be hundreds of jokes that start "A rabbi, a priest, and a Protestant minister ..." Do you know how many Anglicans it takes to screw in a light bulb? At least two—one to change the light bulb, and another to mix the cocktails. One usually makes one's best jokes about one's own denomination. Roman Catholics must have thousands of jokes about nuns and priests. One of our granddaughters knows a jillion Lutheran jokes.

Muslims make jokes about Islam among themselves, too, says Bernard Lewis.[xxi] But perhaps Lewis is talking historically, and the Muslim culture has changed. According to a recent article in *The New York Times Magazine*, stand-up comics in Qatar must not joke about Islam. Comic Mohammed Fahal Kamal says, "We're not used to laughing at ourselves." [xxii] Times are tough indeed when we can't take a joke from ourselves.

Where was I? I started out telling you about the downside to Christianity. (Jokes are more fun to talk about than the downside.) Yes, there is joy. But the joy comes with no guarantees of protection from life's vicissitudes. Christians get laid off from their jobs just like everybody else when their company downsizes or goes bankrupt. It's just that they are down-deep-joyful, in spite of being jobless for the time being.

And just because they are better than they otherwise would be doesn't mean that they are perfect, or easy to live with, so Christian married couples sometimes make each other's lives miserable—but less miserable than if those same two people were unbelievers. Also, God doesn't have any grandchildren--remember?—so sometimes the children of Christians are rebellious and make their parents' lives miserable.

Saving faith does not provide a shield from the troubles of the world. Christians get cancer, and have heart attacks, and miscarriages, and babies born with birth defects. Sometimes the patients of Christian doctors and nurses die. Christians occasionally lose the law suit they were pleading for a client—after all, some of their clients are actually guilty. It's just that they are down-deep-joyful, in spite of the troubles of the world. In spite of their citizenship in Heaven, they live in the world, and are supposed to brighten the corner where they are. Their down-deep-joy in the face of tribulation doesn't necessarily make their life easier.

Sometimes it's quite the opposite. Christians are dying for their faith in Africa, even now: Northern Nigeria, Southern Sudan, Ethiopia, Egypt, Tunisia, Morocco. Islamic mobs attack and kill them, burn them inside their houses and churches, just because they refuse to renounce their belief in Jesus. The same is true in Iraq, Pakistan and Iran. Christians are not allowed to practice their faith in many Islamic countries, or in some Communist countries such as China or Myanmar.

During the same period that Islam and Communism developed a fatal antipathy for Judaism and Christianity, many people living in developed Western countries gave up their belief in Christianity generations willingly, with no external pressure. Many who still call themselves Christian ("I'm not Jewish, for god sake!") are what are called 'hatch, match, and dispatch Christians', using the Church only for christenings, weddings, and funerals. And have you noticed? The church is no longer the event space of choice for these events? Christenings are a non-event for many babies. Their parents have had their wedding at a restaurant, a Bed & Breakfast, a beach, or a Destination Resort. Funerals are more often in funeral homes, if anyone bothers to have one, and are Celebrations of Life, with no mention of God. These superficial Christians would renounce their superficial faith in a New York minute if it were seriously challenged.

Christianity thrives under persecution, which weeds out the fingers-crossed believers and strengthens the faithful. Christians in persecuted parts of the world are praying for persecution of the faith in Europe and America, so that the Church may be purged and strengthened in those lands. I timidly join their prayer, but with fear and trembling for the testing to follow.

In his book *Seven Faith Tribes: Who They Are, What They Believe, and Why They Matter,* George Barna says that Christians are not one but two faith tribes: Casual Christians and Captive Christians.[xxiii] These are not categorized according to denomination (although denomination is an indicator in some cases) but according to their level of commitment to the faith. Barna's Casual Christians are Rice Christians who may in the future acquire saving faith and become Captives. The Captives are voluntary slaves, captivated by Jesus Christ. They believe that supernatural activity (God) impacts the natural world every moment of every day. They honor the past and accept the present, but live for the future, believing that today's troubles simply prepare them for coming trials.[xxiv]

If people choose to bet against God, it is not for us to chastise them. Although we grieve for them, we should defend their prerogative to bet any way they choose. Nevertheless, we should bet on God, either because he created us for that purpose, or so our biochemistry will make nice.

No one wants to dream of being in Hell for all eternity. Lord, we believe. Help thou our unbelief.

10.
Know God

Pascal was concerned about the transformation process, from unbeliever to believer, in his own day, and in this discussion I am concerned about it in ours. In his own natural self, each person resists the existence of the Triune God of Christianity. That such a being not only exists, but also commands our destiny, is abhorrent in the extreme. Pascal affirms that God is infinitely beyond our comprehension, although he reveals some aspects of himself to humanity. We may know *that* God is, Pascal says, without our knowing precisely or completely *what* he is. Nevertheless, Pascal's wager is on this proposition:

> ➢ We ought to bet that God not only exists, but that he cares about us, cares for us, and cares whether or not we believe in him and worship him.

So what should we do to bet? Actually, the measures that Pascal suggests are very much like being a duck. (If it looks like a duck, quacks like a duck, and waddles like a duck, then for all practical purposes, it is a duck.) Pascal says,

You want to find faith and you do not know the road. You want to be cured of unbelief and you ask for the remedy: Learn from those who were once bound like you and who now wager all they have. These are people who know the road you wish to follow, who have been cured of the affliction of which you wish to be cured: follow the way by which they began.

They behaved just as if they did believe, taking holy water, having masses said, and so on. ... Now what harm will come to you from choosing this course? You will be faithful, honest, humble, grateful, full of good works, a sincere, true friend ... I tell you that you will gain even in this life, and that at every step you take along this road you will see that your gain is so certain and your risk so negligible that in the end you will realize that you have wagered on something certain and infinite for which you have paid nothing.[xxvi]

So we should look like a Christian, walk like a Christian, and quack like a Christian, and pretty soon we will be more faithful, honest, humble, grateful, full of good works, obedient, cheerful—sounds like becoming a Scout, doesn't it?

The scientists think that faith-based thoughts may increase "self-monitoring" by evoking the idea of an all-knowing, omnipresent God. ...If God is always watching, we'd better not misbehave.[xxvii]

This is not, of course, trying to fool God into thinking that we believe in him. If we were trying to fool God, then we would need to acknowledge that we already believe in him. Indeed, the ones we're trying to fool are ourselves. We're trying to con ourselves into quacking like Christians, and I admit it's not easy.

For Pascal in seventeenth century France, holy water and masses were the answer. In the United States, or Britain, or Belgium or France or Germany today, those would be the answer for very few people—although they might be the answer for some. The first thing to realize about achieving saving faith, is that no one wants it except those who get it—no matter how much they themselves resist their own effort. Jesus says, "No one can come to me unless the Father draw him." (*John* 6:65) Saving faith is a gift from God. He gives it freely to anyone who asks for it—and to some who don't ask.

The first step for any of us to take is prayer. We might have a place where we can comfortably close the door, get down on our knees, clasp our hands, close our eyes—or not. We can talk to God wherever and in whatever posture we find ourselves. I knew some when I was studying at Oxford who had been a practicing witch, and was converted to Christianity by watching the 1977 Zeffirelli TV miniseries. Her husband was still a warlock, and she had to keep her Bible behind the removable panel of the bathtub. One takes what prayer space one can get. After I knew her, her husband may also have come to belief. That was in about 1980.

God is omnipresent. There is no hiding place from him. A relationship with God is not exactly the same as a relationship with a friend: None of our friends created the world out of nothing.[xxviii] God personally directs each atom in the universe, and we are each made of kajillions of atoms, so he knows and cares about us, every pimple, pore and passion. We have trouble wrapping our minds around even the bare notion of such an enormous intelligence.

Even after Jesus had been crucified and burst from the tomb alive, one of his close disciples, Thomas, doubted the Resurrection. He had not yet seen the risen Jesus, and he said, "Unless I see the nail prints in his hands and touch the wound in his side with my own hand, I cannot believe." It was more than a week later that he was with the other disciples and Jesus appeared among them. Jesus said, "Shalom," and then to Thomas, "Look at my hands, and put your fingers in my side. Don't be unbelieving, but believe." Of course Thomas then believed his own eyes, and said, "My Lord and my God."

We are not eyewitnesses to Jesus' life on earth. We know these things from the testimony of others who were eyewitnesses. Most of us are not eyewitnesses to Woodstock, or Elvis Presley, or the Kennedy assassination. We know about them from people who were eyewitnesses. All we can do is to say, with the man who was asking Jesus to heal his son, "Lord, I would like to believe (I'm beginning to believe). Help my unbelief." (Mark 9:24)

So the first thing we should pray for is to cure our unbelief, by showing us that he exists and is powerful. After such a prayer, he will do that in some unexpected way during the next few days, when we least expect it. He will help our unbelief by giving us an experience of himself. It could be a dream, or a miraculous insight into some quite ordinary thing. It is very important, though, that we recognize him when he shows us that he knows and loves us.

James Martin tells the story about a guy looking for a parking place. He is Best Man for his friend's wedding, and is about to be late. Not a church-goer, he is in such a pickle that he resorts to prayer: "O God, please help me! If you open up a parking place, I'll go to church every Sunday, I'll pray every night, and I'll be kind to everyone I meet." Suddenly a space opens up.

"Oh, never mind, God. I found one." [xxix] How crude! It is only common courtesy to recognize a miracle for what it is. And a little "thank you" might also be apropos.

Then there is the story about a guy who was caught in a flood, and was standing on his roof, surrounded by flood waters. A neighbor came by in a canoe and offered him a ride. "No, thanks, I trust in the Lord to save me." Then another neighbor came in a rowboat, but again he said, "No, thanks, I trust in the Lord to save me." Next came a motor boat, and finally a helicopter. Each time, "No, thanks, I trust in the Lord to save me."

Next thing he knew he was standing there in front of the Pearly Gate, dripping water all over the entry stones while gazing through the gate at the gold pavement. Saint Peter said, "You must show me your saving faith before I can let you go through." He said, "I trusted in the Lord to save me." Pete said, "We sent a canoe, a rowboat, a motor boat and a helicopter. You weren't trusting in the Lord who loves and cares for you. You were trusting in some idol made by human minds. You don't have saving faith." And he hit the button and sprang the trap door. "Bye, by-ee!"

Incidentally, we mustn't get too used to the little miracles, such as parking spaces. After all, God is not our doggie to go fetch. Anyone who is at the Janis Joplin stage of immaturity (O Lord, wontcha buy me a Mercedes Benz) is not very far toward saving faith.

Lord, we believe. Help thou our unbelief.

11.
Is Saving Faith Logical?

*If we submit everything to reason, our religion will be
left with nothing mysterious or supernatural.
If we offend the principles of reason, our religion will be
absurd and ridiculous.*

Blaise Pascal [xxx]

One way that the Lord helps our unbelief is with logic.
I've heard it said that no one is converted by books and
arguments. But I am personally an exception to that,
having come to faith by reading C.S. Lewis's *Mere
Christianity* some fifty years ago. I know other people
who are exceptions, also. God has given us brains with
which to think, and he invites us to exercise that organ
toward attaining saving faith.

I find it difficult to believe something—anything—if I
don't have any evidence to support its accuracy.
Scholars of all stripes have lined up on either side of the
question of whether or not God exists, or whether, on
the other hand, everything that exists does so by pure
accident. Either God is the constant creator of all that
ever has been and ever will be, or he is not. Which side
has the most votes? That is irrelevant to the argument:
We could ever one of us vote either for or against, and
every one of us be wrong. There is, however, evidence
to assist our decision. Since I am of the philosophical
persuasion, and am writing this, it should be obvious
that I have encountered such evidence, and sorted it
toward God's existence. I have had some powerful
help.

For example, Anselm, Archbishop of Canterbury (1033-1109) gives us the evidence of pure, unadulterated logic, using the example of perfection. He illustrates it as a perfect island (whatever that would be). Such a perfect thing can of course be imagined. But if it did not actually exist, its perfection would be thus marred – it cannot be absolutely perfect if it is non-existent, because the addition of existence would add to its perfection. The attributes of God include perfection, and of course it follows that existence is a necessary part of that perfection. Therefore God exists.

That was Anselm's ontological argument: the argument from the science or understanding of being itself. It contends that existence is a property discoverable in the very concept of God. Just after analyzing his argument, and finding the second version of it to be valid, I was accused by colleagues with whom I was having tea to be high on something stronger than tea. I was high on logic.

Then there is the teleological—the goal-oriented—argument. It says that a designer is required to get to the present state of affairs. If the universe were left up to chance, chaos would be the result. The more we learn about the universe, at both macro and micro levels, the more implausible it seems for it to be the result of chance. The alternative is the Designer we call God. This argument also is valid. It was ignored for centuries because philosopher David Hume discredited an inaccurate version of it. Scholars habitually give inaccurate examples of somrthing they want to refute. Cowards!

Intelligent Design is the more recent exercise of the argument from design, and is stronger than its predecessors because its science is more advanced. It is easy to discredit these days, because people with more vigor than rigor have hopped onto its bandwagon and present their own versions. They present the opponents of Intelligent Design with Straw Men that are easy to knock down. We must be cautious when we wander into this minefield, but there is strong evidence here for God, Designer and Creator, despite the Straw Men that are easy to topple.

There has never been a dearth of philosophers who are eager to say that all the arguments for God are mistaken, for one reason or another. For example, Immanuel Kant (1704-1824) says that existence is not a proper predicate. He says that you can prove all sorts of things about all sorts of things – you can say that the wagon is red, or has four wheels, or that it has a black handle, but to say that the wagon exists is simply not a meaningful thing to say. But Kant's objection is balderdash to most real people, and even to many other philosophers. (Disclosure: I have taught philosophy to college students at several institutions.)

For example, let Kant tell it to a child on Christmas morning. Is that Flexible Flyer sled he has been envisioning under the Christmas tree just as good non-existent as existent? Herr Professor Kant, we all beg to differ: sleds and dolls and diamond rings and fur coats and power tools and golf clubs are much better for being predicated as existent, rather than just figments of the imagination. We want them not only existent, but wrapped beautifully, tied with a bow, and marked "with love from Santa". We really like existent . . . except, of course, when it is Hell.

Some philosophers also attack language about God as not publicly true, simply because it is God-talk. Some scholars have tried to improve the world by ruling all God-talk out of court as neither true nor false – just some kind of word soup (one step up from alphabet soup). Avowed atheist Robert W. Funk says, for example, "We must reckon with a deep crisis in god talk and replace it with talk about whether the universe has meaning and whether human life has purpose."[xxxi] He and others claim that nothing said within religion can be true in the generally accepted sense of the word 'true', because religious talk is not falsifiable. That is, there is no situation in which it is not True in some ineffable sense. Funk and company assume that all discussions about God use language in this way.

I maintain that they are mistaken in making such a blanket assessment of God-talk. There are at least three kinds of truth, all variously used in God-talk, only one of which succumbs to the fuzzy meaninglessness Funk wants to ascribe to it. Sometimes truth is . . .

> . . . actually true-with-a-lower-case-'t'. That is, publicly, objectively true for everybody, and (in principle, at least) *verifiable or falsifiable;*

> . . . wonderfully-True-with-an-upper-case-'T'. That is, *inspiring and elusive and not verifiable even in principle except by personal experience;*

. . . relatively true, that is, *true relative to whatever circumstances in which it is used*, such as games or social conventions, or local laws.

All three are used in God-talk quite legitimately in various different circumstances.

An example of *verifiable* truth is a phone listing. We dial the number listed, and the right person answers. Voila! If someone else answers and says "wrong number", it is false. Someone goofed.

The *elusive* Truth is illustrated beautifully in a paper presented at a musicology conference I recently attended. The presenter's thesis was that the music of U2 (a pop music group) was an example of Barthian Prayer. (Karl Barth was a Swiss theologian, 1886-1968.) The presenter showed what he meant by saying that U2's music is sincere and is the work of their soul, and he considered those to be the requirements for Barthian prayer. In the Question and Answer period following his presentation, the audience members seemed to be concerned with what were the corollaries of this interpretation. Is the music of other groups also Barthian Prayer? Yes. Does the content matter? No. The words? No, it is still Barthian Prayer. Is the product of other sorts of artists also Barthian Prayer? Yes. Does the subject matter? No. Is the product that an engineer makes when he designs something also Barthian Prayer? Yes. What about what a teacher does? That's Barthian Prayer, too. The upshot seems to be that whatever someone does with sincerity this presenter regarded as Barthian Prayer.

Whether or not this is an adequate interpretation of what Barth himself would have acknowledged as his own version, it illustrates what philosophers object to about much God-Talk: It has no falsifiability. That is, the presenter here seemed to have no sincere human activity that was not Barthian Prayer. I wondered afterward what he might have said about a murderer performing an exquisitely gruesome murder. Is he, too, engaged in Barthian Prayer? In what sense does God love all the people of the world, and accept them just as they are, without one plea? Is there no limit to those for whom he shed his blood upon the cross? Many theologies get caught up in Elusive Truth and fail to sort out such issues.

The classic illustration of fatuous talk that claims to represent the sincere Christian believer is in a paper written in 1945.[xxxii], [15] Here Anthony Flew gives an exaggerated example of how Christians have made a virtue of believing, no matter what evidence is formulated against the object of their belief. I call the basis for this kind of belief Truth with a capital 'T', to indicate that it differs from ordinary truth, which is based on evidence.

Flew illustrates with a situation in which two men come upon a beautiful patch of woods, and one claims that there must be a gardener who made it so beautiful, like the Christian claim that God made the universe. His companion says that it just happened to grow like that,

---

[15] It is discussed in greater depth in my forthcoming book, *A Philosophical Overture: Academic Legends*.

because there is no evidence of a gardener – no matter what they do, they can't catch a gardener at work.

To a degree, the critics of God-talk are right. It is like the "U2's music is Barthian Prayer" claim above, in which nothing counts as not-Barthian-Prayer. If it makes no sense to say that so-and-so is false, then it makes no sense to claim that it is true in any ordinary sense of 'true'.

An example of *relative* truth can be rules in a game or a school or a community: "Curfew here is 11 pm sharp." "Detergent bottles are not recyclable." "Spades are trump."

But I maintain here that even though some God-talk is True only ineffably, but not falsifiably and so not publicly true, other God-talk *is* falsifiable and so it is indeed true – publicly true. Many of the miracles in the Bible are just such example of truth-with-a-small-'t'. The people telling about them know that they are talking about out-of-the-ordinary events. "Jesus turned water into wine." What a useful thing to do! We should harness that talent and use it for making wine. But No, it was a one-off miracle. The person writing about it, John the disciple and gospel writer, was an eyewitness to the event. After seeing many supposedly impossible sleights of hand performed by magicians, most of us are inclined to be skeptical about such things.

Do we believe the story, or not? John is saying, "If you had been there and seen it with your own eyes, you would have had no choice but to believe it." Without resorting to setting them as hypotheses and testing these, the unbeliever would probably react to them as Alice[16] does:

> Alice laughed: "There's no use trying," she said; "one can't believe impossible things." "I daresay you haven't had much practice," said the Queen. "When I was younger, I always did it for half an hour a day. Why, sometimes I've believed as many as six impossible things before breakfast."[xxxiii]

Lewis Carroll is making fun of Christians here. The central tenets of the faith include the claim that Jesus was born of a Virgin, the miracles he and later his disciples performed, and the central miracle, that he was killed by the Romans, buried, and three days later he came back to life, met with his friends, ate fish, taught his disciples, and after forty days of this, descended bodily to heaven—a phenomenon known in the Church by the code word 'Resurrection'. Are these Lewis Carol's six impossible things that one might practice believing before breakfast? I suspect they are.

Are they Anthony Flew's classic impossible God-talk? I suspect they are. Is Flew's objection to god-talk well-founded? Actually, it turns out not to be. Discussion about these things is falsifiable, hence perfectly capable of being disproved. Some God-talk is unfalsifiable—it can be neither proved nor disproved. It is neither true nor false. But these historical events are in principle capable of being disproved. And lots of people have tried to disprove them, but have not succeeded.

---

[16] This from scorner Lewis Carroll in *Alice in Wonderland*. As usual, the Devil has all the best lines.

Subconsciously, when we look for truth we are looking for a match between what we understand about the object of discussion, and the way we perceive the world to be. In this case, is there a god out there somewhere that matches what Christianity calls God? The relation of truth to belief seems to be cumulative. If we are told something lots of times, and we are never led to believe that there is any reason to doubt it, we are inclined to believe it.

Flew here seems to assume that Christian belief is a result of repetition without any healthy skepticism thrown in. He neglects to pay attention to what the Bible actually says, and what Christians actually attests.

Physicist John Polkinghorne warns us that we should not condemn ourselves to thinking that we have said all we can say about music, when science has enabled us to note that it is vibrations in the air. [xxxiv] Information about vibrations in the air is falsifiable, but we can say much more about music that is both true and True, and some things about it that are only relatively true. Some of what we might say is falsifiable—that it is in the key of D, or that it was written in 1812. Some of what we say about it is ineffable—what emotions it evokes in ourselves, perhaps. Some of what we say about particular music (perhaps an Indian raga or an Italian aria) is relative to whichever culture generates that particular music. Hence what we say about music can be true, True, or relative.

The same can be said of god-talk. Some of what we can say is culture-relative, some is ineffable Truth, and some is falsifiable, as historical or otherwise measurable public truth.

Without this analysis, however, many Modernist philosophers (16th to the 20th centuries in general, although some people are still stuck in Modernism even into the 21st century) take the position that religious talk should be evaluated as poetry or fiction is evaluated, because they assume that all three— poetry, fiction, and religion—lack falsifiability.

Lord, we believe. Help thou our unbelief.

12.
Truth or Consequences

"Beauty is truth, and truth beauty"[17]
Hogwash!
For some people, truth is not even beautiful,
much less beauty itself, but an object of abject fear.

In claiming that *"Beauty is truth, and truth beauty"*, Keats gives us a perfect example of poetic Truth-with-a-capital-T. Yes, there is some ephemeral relation of truth to beauty. But it has to be given and received as poetic insight rather than as a proposition for which there is evidence, or even potential evidence. We can all think of counter-instances where the truth is ugly indeed. Although some people would want to use the word 'true' to describe some poetry, or fiction, or passage of Scripture, because it is very meaningful to them, they would be a bit sloppy doing that. We should not insist that poetic Truth is publicly true in the same sense that a correct phone listing is true. Here we leave aside relative truths and the Truths of insight and poetry for the moment and concentrate on objective truths.

Here I am in danger of insulting the sensibilities of many of my friends. For example, when I say that "Jesus is the Way, the Truth, and the Life" is not true, following this rule, is not to say it is false, either. It is not falsifiable as it stands, so one must say that it is 'True' with a capital 'T to describe it. On the other

---

17 John Keats, "Ode On a Grecian Urn"

hand, Christianity says that Jesus rose from the dead. I argue, elsewhere, that this is true. Here I merely assert that this is falsifiably true (or false), and is a theoretically testable event in public history. Falsifiability and testability are useful distinctions for objective truth, because they confront head-on the issue of whether or not an assertion is either true or false. Either he did or he didn't rise from the dead, and it is true or false for anybody and everybody, whether they care to believe it or not.

Falsifiability is the generally accepted criterion for public truth, and we accept it here in this present conversation. For example, most propositions in mathematics, physics, history, biology, geography and such can be demonstrated in principle to be either true or false. Consider the following propositions: '5 + 3 = 8', 'acceleration due to gravity is 32 feet per second per second', 'Louis XIV of France married his mistress, Mme. De Maintenon, in 1684', 'the DNA molecule is a coiled double helix', and 'Jerusalem is southwest of ancient Babylon'. If any of these statements were false, that fact could be demonstrated. But no proposition can be true in any publicly verifiable sense of 'true' with a lower case 't' if its negation is not false. Let me emphasize that, because it is the standard used here and elsewhere:

No proposition can be true if its negation is not false.

It follows from this that if it is true that 'acceleration due to gravity is 32 feet per second per second', and 'Louis XIV married Mme. de Maintenon in 1684' and so on are true, then their negations are false. On a true/false test, if you marked the sentence 'Louis XIV married Mme. de Maintenon in 1684' as false, you goofed. You cannot protest to the teacher that everything is relative. Statements about historical events are true or false with a lower case 't'. The only way you might win that argument would be to present applicable evidence against the marriage. The same is the case for Jesus' resurrection from death. It is not enough to say that either assertion—about Jesus or Louis—is simply poetic language and hence neither true nor false.

On the other hand, Narnia (which is a place in C.S. Lewis's fiction) is neither southwest of Never-Never Land (which is a place in J.M. Barrie's play, *Peter Pan*) nor is it **not** southwest of Never-Never Land. Such claims about Narnia and Never-Never Land are simply not in the realm of public truth, no matter how beloved they are. One might claim that Narnia, for example, is a True place (with a capital T), but it would be a mistake to say that it is a true place, like Jerusalem or Babylon or Tallahassee is a true—in the sense of 'actual'—place.

In the hymn "Jerusalem the Golden with milk and honey blessed", Jerusalem is a True place. When the Book of *Revelation* speaks of Babylon (Rev. 14:8, 16:19, 17:1 – 18:24), it is talking about a True (and nasty) Babylon rather than the Babylon that was northeast of Jerusalem. And when Bing Crosby sings that Tallahassee is "the Southland at its best," it is of course True. But none of this is true with a lower case 't'. If someone claimed they were, he'd be talking nonsense. This is not to say that the assertions are false, but merely that they are not objectively, falsifiably true.

One way to understand what Flew is trying to say is to attempt to find what he would regard as counting against it, or as being incompatible with its truth.[xxxv] In 1955 Flew was speaking for the atheist position, implying that (all) God-talk is nonsense.[18] But he was mistaken. The heart of Christianity is full of lower-case plain, ordinary statements, which can in principle be falsified or verified. It is also full of believers who have resisted faith with all their human strength, and in the long run came to believe that the central claims of Christianity are true—lower-case.

Among them is St. Paul, who wrote,

> If there is no resurrection of the dead, then our preaching is in vain, and your faith is in vain. We of all men are most to be pitied. But in fact Christ has been raised from the dead. (1 Corinthians 15:13-20)

Paul is echoed by the French Dominican biblical scholar and archaeologist Roland de Vaux, who is quoted as saying that "if the historical faith of Israel is not founded in history, such faith is erroneous, and therefore, our faith is also."[xxxvi] De Vaux also says,

> [W]e must insist that Israel's religion was an historical religion, and that the faith of Israel was based on God's interventions in the history of his people.[xxxvii]

18:38[18] He has since written a book entitled *There is a God,* having come to a theistic mind-set in the meanwhile. There is a question as to whether he came to saving faith before his death. Only God knows.

These statements are echoed by Christians throughout the world and throughout the ages, who recite the ancient creeds: "I believe . . . [that] Jesus was crucified under Pontius Pilate; he suffered death and was buried, and on the third day he rose again . . . etc." (The Nicene Creed)

This is part of the Scandal of Particularity that is at the heart of Christianity. Jesus was a particular person, born into a particular people with a particular culture and history. It is ineffably True that he is "the Word that became flesh in a given time and place."[xxxviii] It is plain, ordinary true (or false) that Jesus was born in Bethlehem. And it is plain, ordinary true (or false) that he was killed dead on the cross, was buried, and then was resurrected from the dead and was seen by well over five hundred eyewitnesses after his resurrection. The Christian Faith rests on its factual historicity, and fails if its historical particulars are historically false.

These statements make Judeo-Christianity, unlike most other religions, falsifiable. Christian believers must be willing, with Paul, to forego their faith if it can be demonstrated unequivocally that Jesus was not resurrected from the dead. They must be willing to give up their Sunday-go-to-meeting clothes, their hymns praising Jesus, the crosses around their necks, everything in their lives that affirms that Jesus of Nazareth is the Incarnate God the Son, if it can be shown that there is no resurrection of the dead. But Paul goes on to say,

. . . in fact, Christ has been raised from the dead.

Paul himself did not see the risen Jesus. But he had it on myriad first-person eyewitness testimonies from Peter and the hundreds of other disciples who were eyewitnesses to the risen Jesus--who could testify that Jesus had been raised from the dead.[19] Paul was willing to die in defense of this testimony. In fact he did die for his belief, as did thousands of other Christian martyrs. Christians continue to die for its truth even into the twenty-first century.

The possibility that the core claims of Christianity are false is historically improbable to the nth degree. If we are ready to believe that Alexander crossed the Hellespont, why are we not ready to believe that Moses and company crossed the Red Sea dry shod, and that Jesus rose from the dead? All three are attested by many witnesses.[20] Hence, there is truth, public and true for everybody whether they agree with it, believe it, like it or not.

If we bet against God's activities in human history—and whether or not he exists—we are betting against something well-attested. It's like betting against your opponent's having the ace of spades when ten of your friends are standing behind him looking at his hand, and saying, "Yes, he has the ace of spades." You'd be crazy to bet against it!

---

[19] The fact that Paul here is focusing not on Christ's resurrection, but on the doctrine of general resurrection of all believers is irrelevant here. He attests Christ crucified, resurrected, and enthroned. That is what makes any doctrine of the general resurrection possible.

[20] See *Matthew* 28, *Mark* 16, *Luke* 24, *John* 20 and 21.

Betting against God also causes a bad result that we ourselves can witness: we don't experience the joy that a saving faith would bring us during our cruise of life, and it would cause us at death to experience an eternal Hell. But if God exists, and our saving faith is in God the Creator and Preserver of all that is, Almighty, All-knowing, etc., then there will probably be something added: We will not only have joy in this life, but will go to Heaven when we die. See?! Christians have more fun!

And are more intelligent than they would otherwise be. One of the first things I did after I became a believer was to take an IQ test, because I had always labored under the supercilious assumption that the only reason anybody could believe all that Jesus stuff was a serious case of stupidity. But then I discovered the Christian Underground—the subset of church members who actually believe all that stuff—and found out that the Christian life is a constant celebration: but not necessarily in the sense that most people understand 'celebration'. I know lots of intelligent Christians, and a fair number of unintelligent unbelievers. Back when I took time to be active in Mensa, there was a lively group of Christian Mensans.

So. If God exists, and we bet that he exists, what is our gain? Joy in him now and forevermore. What do we stand to lose? Nothing, really. We can read the Sunday *New York Times* on Sunday afternoons, if we still want to.

If God doesn't exist, and we bet that he exists, what is our gain? Apparently, the same things we gained if he does exist. We see that coming to a saving faith in Jesus gives us joy here in this life on earth. And evidence from Near Death Experiences indicates that betting on God gives us a dream experience in our dying moments that has a property of seeming endless, and is an endless bliss in the presence of God, praising him and rejoicing in him forever, whereas if we bet against God this same endless final dream mimics Hell.

If God does not exist, and we bet that he *does* exist, we gain the joy on earth that saving faith brings, even when that faith in a mirage. In life we would experience the joy of worshiping that God-like figment of our collective imagination together with thousands of others stricken with similar imaginations. We will be joined by those born with Godly tone-deafness or dystonia, who have chosen to undergo Deep Brain Stimulation to overcome this defect in their inherited DNA. As we die, our synaptic activity will lock us into a dream loop of Heaven.

If God does not exist and we bet that God does not exist, you'd think we would be home free. But we are not. There is still that pesky joy that we get when we bet that God exists, so even if he does not, if we bet against him we miss out on the joy. And don't forget the Near Death Experiences. So even if he does not exist, if we bet against him we will forfeit the joy on earth and endless Heavenly bliss that comes with saving faith. Even if God does not exist and we bet against him, as we die our brains lock into the other endless dream loop—we smell the sulphur, we feel the heat, we hear the demon laughter, and there is no escape. The same dream endlessly repeated into an infernal and eternal phantasmagoria of horrors.

Is there a gain for betting for the non-existence of a non-existent God? Maybe we gain time that we would have wasted on worshiping God, or supposedly doing things for him or his minions. But no, we don't really gain anything by not worshiping a non-existent God that is not offset by its benefits.

And remember, we can read the Sunday *New York Times* on Sunday afternoon.

We can sympathize with Alice in finding it hard to believe something we think is impossible, and people who believe that God is non-existent find themselves in this predicament. Of course, they don't see it as a predicament: They either are so set against belief that they resist belief in spite of anything, or they haven't learned about the arguments for his existence.

The former has a habit of unbelief similar to those people who refuse to believe that the Nazi government deliberately slaughtered thirteen million people they considered to be undesirable, including Gypsies, believing Christians, and six million Jews. There are others who refuse to believe that airplanes destroyed the twin towers of the World Trade Center in 2001. Still others refuse to believe that Elvis is really truly dead and gone. There is no help that I know of other than fervent prayer for those whose minds are completely closed.

We can help the latter by recommending books that give lucid scientific and logical evidence that the universe did not create itself, and that the creator fits the attributes that Judeo-Christianity has assigned to God. An open mind is a marvelous benefit to its owner. There was a time when I thought that the fool, who says in his heart that there is no God, might have a point. Why should I believe all this Christian nonsense? The Jewish singer who was paid to sing in our church choir must have thought it was nonsense, but he had his paycheck as an excuse for being there. I was volunteering my time. If Christianity is all a pretty fiction, my Sunday mornings would be better spent at home in my bathrobe with a pot of good coffee and the Sunday *New York Times*.

So I asked one of our clergymen for suggested Advent reading, and C.S. Lewis dragged me into belief, kicking at the goad. Lewis tells us that it is Christianity's very nonsense that makes it plausible. Nobody would have made up such preposterous tom-foolery. Take the Virgin Birth. If Mary didn't have a husband when she conceived, why call attention to the fact? She could have gotten away with it—after all, she and Joseph were already betrothed, and nobody would have thought anything of it if they jumped the gun by a few weeks.

Lewis points out that the Virgin Birth is not the sort of thing people would make up. Athena was the Virgin Goddess, but not a mother. There are demi-gods in other religions, but none like Jesus, fully God and fully man. So why bring up Virgin Birth at all? Because it is true. It happened as advertised, and it is marvelous and miraculous, complete with angels.

"And what about all that Resurrection business? Jesus didn't really rise from the dead, did he? The really Progressive Christian theologians get it right, don't they, when they say that the Resurrection actually took place in the hearts and minds of the apostles?"

No, actually, they don't get it right. How could the disciples have invented the Resurrection? The Romans posted soldiers to guard the tomb so the Christians couldn't steal the body. The Christians went looking for the body, and it was already gone. What happened to it? If the Romans did away with the body themselves, then when rumors of Resurrection started, the Roman government could have quashed the rumors by producing the dead body. So the Romans didn't have the body.

The Jewish rulers were glad to get rid of that troublemaker Jesus: If they had had the body, they certainly would have produced it, to prove that the Resurrection didn't happen. The Christians couldn't have had the body either. Their stealing the body is what the Roman guards were guarding against. It would have been impossible for those grieving friends to move the stone and steal the body without disturbing the guards. Let's hypothesize that enough of them to heft the stone had come to the site, drugged the guards, moved the stone, and stolen the body. There are several things wrong with this picture.

First, the guards would have snitched on them. Second, there would have to have been enough disciples to manhandle the stone away from the mouth of the tomb. A group that large would have not been able to keep their shenanigans a secret from the other mourners. Third, if the disciples had had the body, they would not have simply re-buried it. What would have been the purpose of stealing the body only to rebury it? It already had a very good tomb. A dead body is no good to them if not to venerate it, and there is no veneration tradition. Moreover, deception is not compatible with holiness. Allison observes that the transformation of these timid and fearful friends of Jesus into confident, committed, and courageous witnesses and martyrs is nothing short of miraculous. It was the Resurrection that transformed them, not they who conjured up the Resurrection.

If the disciples had stolen the body, they would have had to deceptively keep it hidden, without giving it a proper burial and without venerating it, for the rest of their lives. They would have had to keep their grizzly secret while their fellow disciples were making up stories about Jesus sightings, all the while knowing that he was dead. When the persecutions began, they could have saved their own skins and the lives of their friends by 'fessing up and producing the corpse. But no, they went to the ends of the earth preaching the good news that Jesus had risen from the dead.

Finally they went to their own deaths in the Coliseum, or as Nero's torches, singing praises to Jesus, proclaiming the good news about their risen Lord, which they would have known to be a lie. Committees don't keep secrets. Somebody leaks the truth. Somebody confesses to Rome or to the Jewish authorities. Somebody outside the Committee finds out about it. Somebody smells the unburied body.

No. The tomb was empty. There was no dead body for Christians to worship, or for Sadducees to gloat over, or for Romans to vilify.

And then Jesus started showing up in his brand new Resurrection Body. The new body was recognizable as Jesus to those who had known his old regular body, but even they often didn't recognize him immediately. Nor did the new body have the same limitations as our old bodies. He could eat fish – did so on at least two occasions—so presumably that new body could swallow and digest, unlike your ordinary run-of-the-mill ghost. He could show up anywhere: Walls were no barrier. There were lots of eyewitnesses to his post-Resurrection appearances: his close disciples saw him many times, and as many as five hundred people saw him at one time. When these events were written in the gospels and letters in the New Testament, many of those eyewitnesses were still around to dispute any inaccuracies in the written record, if there had been inaccuracies. What nonsense to suggest that his post-Resurrection appearances were figments of imagination.

If these people were not seeing a resurrected Jesus, they were experiencing mass hysteria. They certainly thought they were seeing Jesus alive again after he had died on the cross. There is no accurate record anywhere of that sort of mass hysteria. That is not what happened. Those people saw the risen Jesus talk with them in a crowd of five hundred, talk with them up close and personal, eat with them, tell them how to catch fish, and challenge his friend Thomas to feel his scars from the crucifixion. They were eyewitnesses to the risen Jesus.

Well, I was not an eyewitness to Jesus' Resurrection body. But I am an eyewitness to the miracle of joy that men and women experience when they receive the gift of saving faith: when they come to believe in impossible events that happened two thousand years ago. When we make a commitment to that belief, and publicly declare that commitment, the resurrected Jesus does something in our lives that brings us great joy.

I am an eyewitness to the joy of suppers with other Christians, of studying the Bible together, of taking meals to those who need them, of stapling and stuffing Sunday bulletins with the Press Club. Not everyone does Press Club, or sings in the choir, or arranges flowers, or cooks for the men's breakfasts, or preaches, or visits the shut-ins, or scrubs the toilets. Everyone gets fellowship and joy from what they do. This kind of joy is a powerful motivator.

Lord, we believe. Help thou our unbelief.

13.
Isaiah's Log Revisited

A man went into the forest and cut a log.
He brought it home and cut it in two.
With one piece he made a fire and cooked his supper.
With the other piece he carved an idol.
Then he worshiped the idol, thanking it for his supper,
begging it to provide food for tomorrow, to heal his boils,
and to grant him a son.
Was he an idiot, or what?
Isaiah 44:9-20 (with great liberties)

Beautiful Dreamer: OK, I think I get it: Saving faith or belief in Jesus is what gets us all these wonderful benefits: Joy, happiness, loving kindness and all that here on earth, and everlasting blessedness, actually taking pleasure in doing nothing but singing praise to God before the Heavenly throne, for all eternity after death. "But how do I know real Christianity from all that other stuff out there? Is there a secret handshake or password? What if I bet on the wrong game, or root for the wrong team, like the guy who trusted in God to save him? Where can I find authentic Christianity?

Pascal II: Nowhere. It does not exist. This is a fallen world, and there is no human actuality that is the Church, the whole Church, and nothing but the Church, so help me, God. But there are many local churches that are given the grace to exemplify authentic Christianity more or less. However … hooray! you are obviously on your way to glory! …You are right, there are traps to avoid. And the most dangerous aspect of these traps is this. The people who are trying to spring them on us are caught in the traps themselves. They are sincere and mostly innocent of guile—unfortunately, some of them think that guile is a virtue when it is on behalf of bringing us into their religion. They don't realize that they themselves are caught in the trap they are trying to spring on us.

But who am I to say what God gives them credit for? There's the story about St. Peter showing a new arrival around heaven. They stroll around the streets of gold, past great throngs of people singing lustily, various versions of what seems to be all the same song: "Holy, Holy, Holy is the Lord of Hosts!" Sometimes as they pass a door, Peter tiptoes, and puts his finger to his lips for silence. Finally the Newbie asks why. "Oh, some of our groups think they are the only ones here. We wouldn't want to spoil their eternity!"

Jesus said, "In the Father's household are many rooms. I go to prepare a place for you." Did he go to prepare a place for everybody, no matter what they believe and profess? No, he says that he is our judge, and on the Day of Judgment, he will separate the sheep from the goats. And we don't want to get caught with the goats. We need to pray for all of them, because if anyone is caught up in one of these fake forms of religion they are just as lost as were Joe, Bitsy, and our Beautiful Dreamers were, until they came to saving faith. And we also pray for our own fallibility. We may be wrong. But there are pretty clear and dependable guidelines.

Some years ago, an Episcopal bishop compared himself—with graduate degrees, author of scholarly books, and recipient of many honors—to a little old lady who had not finished high school. Yet she understood intuitively the theological consequences of God's sovereignty better than he did. He came to belief in God's sovereignty—in the process of a renewed empowerment of the Holy Spirit—sometime after he was already a bishop. He likened the experience with knowing a country at first hand, as compared to knowing it from studying its maps. He suddenly found himself actually in the country. The uneducated little old lady had been traveling around that country—God's Sovereignty—for many years, and knew it like we know the way to our usual super market. Coming to saving faith is like being parachuted into a land you may have been learning about from studying its maps and language out of books and atlases, and finally experiencing it and knowing it like the little old lady.

I love maps. Before I visit places, I like to study a map of it, imagining what it will actually be like. Sometimes, though, my map study isn't up to snuff. We once traveled by car from the south of England, to Cherbourg, France, driving off the channel ferry in the middle of the night, and realized that we didn't have a map of any sort—no road map, no Michelin guide book, nothing. We drove around in the pitch black dark, trying to go south but not knowing the territory well enough from the signposts at intersections to even drive in the right direction

That is how many people find themselves with respect to the sovereignty of God. They are driving around in the dark without a map, and the signposts they see are no help at all. What I'm trying to offer here is a very rudimentary map of the land. Some religions pose as salvation, when they have no power to save. They are idols made by human minds, and not by God.

Here are several questions to ask, to see if you are in a church that practices and encourages genuine Christianity:

- o Does it proclaim Jesus as the Christ, the Son of the Living God, fully God and fully man?
- o Are their Scriptures the ones handed down through the ages from the Patriarchs of Judaism to the Apostles of Jesus, and from them to us?
- o Are the beliefs handed down to us from the Patriarchs: from the God of Abraham, Isaac, and Jacob?
- o Does it say that Jesus was born to the Virgin Mary, that he taught about the Kingdom of God, healed the sick and worked other miracles, was crucified, died, was buried, rose from the dead, ascended to the Father in Heaven, and sent the Holy Spirit to guide and protect us?

Most of the religions of mankind offer ways for us to climb up to the god, or nirvana, or paradise. They are far removed from Christianity, which along with Judaism features a God who is Sovereign over history, enters history, and encounters mankind as particular people where we are. Other religions seem to be primarily focused on idols made by human hands—and by human minds. Three of the major world religions are based on a tradition of God reaching out to a man, Abram of Ur, in the Tigris and Euphrates valley in about 2000 BC. God told Abraham to leave Ur and go to a place that he would show him. So Abram left Ur, and went (eventually) to Canaan. There he had two sons, Ishmael and Isaac. The Arabs are descended from Ishmael, and the Jews from Isaac. Judaism is the religion that was given to the Jews through Abram (who later became Abraham), Isaac, Jacob, and Moses, who came along about 300 years after Jacob and wrote the first five books of the Bible, telling the story of God's interaction with mankind, and specifically with the Jews, God's chosen people.

Judaism and Christianity were given to the world by God, who kept coming to the Jewish people, nudging them (us) to get their (our) act together. They (we) kept wandering out of the straight and narrow, either ignoring him altogether, making idols they (we) thought would take better care of them (us), or becoming so fanatic as to make each other rules that nobody could possibly keep. After all, it's hard to pay close attention to a god you can't see, even when He sends prophets to guide.

So God took on flesh and was born as a Jewish baby about 2000 years after the time of Abraham. He lived and taught and was put to death as Jewish. Then he rose from the dead and told his disciples to take the news of the Kingdom of God to the ends of the earth. By that time the whole Mediterranean world spoke Greek, so the Hebrew land Messiah the Jews were looking for became the Christ, which means Messiah in Greek. His followers became called Christians.

The standard of real Christianity is its statement of belief: the ancient creeds (a word which comes from the Latin word 'credo', "I believe".) These are faith statements. They are not different from one another in significant ways, but through history each attempts to clarify the earlier ones. They probably started with the original statement, "Jesus is Lord." Then they clarified who they mean by 'Jesus', and what they mean by 'Lord', and what the meaning of the word 'is' is, in this context. But not all religious belief systems we are offered these days are the One True Faith. How do we know that they are wrong?

Compare the historical claims of another faith against the historical claims of Christianity, the texts of Christianity and Judeo-Christianity with the texts of another faith. Judeo-Christianity is undergirded time after time, instance after instance, by confirmations of archaeology and paleography (ancient writings) of Judeo-Christianity. For examples of this, see the bibliography at the end – particularly the work of Kenneth A. Kitchen's *The Reliability of the Old Testament*, F.F. Bruce's *New Testament History*. The foundations of some other faiths have no such confirmations. Its historical past may go back less than two hundred years. Getting the wrong answer to the question, 'Who is Jesus?' gets everything else completely out of whack.

Judaism is the faith that is closest to Christianity. Jesus, the Christ and the Rock on whom Christianity is grounded, was Jewish. Christianity's Scriptures includes the entire Jewish Torah (Law), Nevi'im (Prophets), and Ketuvim (Writings): the Tanach. This is called by Christians the 'Old Testament'. Christianity adds to that a much shorter collection of writings: the four gospels, the letters mostly of Paul but also of three other disciples, and the Revelation of John. Much of the text in these Christian Scriptures includes quotations from the Jewish Scriptures.

Again, the crucial issue is the person of Jesus. He is regarded by Judaism as a prophet, but his divinity is rejected. Christianity claims that Jesus is the expected Jewish Messiah--God's Anointed One. Judaism is still expecting the Messiah, and every now and then a Jewish man is thought by many to be the Messiah. But none except Jesus have fulfilled or can fulfill the prophecies in the Jewish Scriptures that tell what the Messiah's characteristics will be. For example, the Messiah will be a descendant of David. Jesus is a descendant of David. Who else? No one knows. Ever since the archives of the Temple in Jerusalem were destroyed by the Romans, it is impossible for anyone to show that he exemplifies all of those predictions. Those were fulfilled in the life and ministry of Jesus of Nazareth.

Can anyone prove that? No, not about Jesus nor about anyone else. The records were destroyed by the Romans when they sacked and burned the Temple in 70 AD. But the claims about his fulfilling them date from before the destruction of the Temple, and at that time, proof of his lineage and birthplace were there for anyone to see. The claim's authenticity was not an issue.

The central issue is, of course, 'What is the god of this faith?' The earliest Christian statement of this seems to have been, "Jesus is Lord." Then they clarified further, and emphasized. So we have a historical upside-down pyramid of faith statements building on 'Jesus is Lord' through the Apostles Creed and the Nicene Creed (the two creeds used in many churches these days) to the Chalcedon Statement of Definition, and Athanasius' Creed, to the Reformation period statements, such as the Thirty-Nine Articles of the Anglican Communion, and the Westminster Confession of the Presbyterians. The Church Fathers did a thorough job; we need no further clarification. We just need to adhere to the Faith as they set it out. We can speak of them collectively as 'the creed'. It is not the recitation of the creed in church that is important so much as the tenets to which it attests. Many authentically Christian churches don't habitually have everyone recite the creed together as part of their ritual, but their theology agrees with its tenets.

And then there is Christianity Lite. What's new in Christianity Lite? Crossed fingers.[21] If one says the creed with fingers crossed figuratively behind one's back, and with a clear conscience, there is something wrong with one's conscience. Why say it at all if you're going to cross your fingers? Some congregations don't. They recite something from another religion, or something a local poet or committee made up. "Well, I like the trappings and other perks with going to church. But all that theology stuff is merely metaphorical." No, it is not merely metaphorical. It is solid, verifiable-or-falsifiable truth as in chapter 7.

---

[21] In the culture in which I grew up, if you cross your fingers when you say something that is not true, the crossed fingers allow you not to count the falsehood as a lie. Crazy, no? We also could say 'tickalox' and the friend would be locked into wherever he was until we came and said, 'un-tickalox'. Some spells are powerful, especially those in children's games.

In saying the creed, the Christian swears to belief in a very well-attested piece of history. Jesus was born, taught, died on the cross on Friday, was buried; then on Sunday morning when some women arrived at the tomb, he had been resurrected. The tomb was empty; the burial cloths were in a peculiar heap.

And then Jesus began turning up to talk with his friends. He kept showing up with friends and disciples for forty days before he took his final leave, telling them that he's leaving, but that whoever confesses him and is baptized will be given saving faith, and that he is not leaving them as orphans. He is sending them the Holy Spirit to guide and empower them. He also had told them that he will return, coming on the clouds of Heaven, but in the meanwhile they are all to be his witnesses to the ends of the earth.

Only those who have a prejudice against miracles in general and the Resurrection miracle in particular, are unable to follow this historical narrative to its logical conclusion: The Resurrection happened. We say in the Nicene Creed, '. . . *He ascended into Heaven and is seated at the right hand of the Father. He will come again in glory to judge the living and the dead, and his kingdom will have no end.'* We also say, '*Christ has died, Christ is risen, Christ will come again.*'

Christianity Lite answers that it is fatuous to say that Christ has died: of course he did. Everybody who lived then has died. Christianity Lite says that 'Christ is risen' happened in the hearts and minds of the Faithful: the Church is the Risen Christ. But they fail to acknowledge their logical blunder: the 'Christ' who has died is not the same 'Christ' who 'lives in the hearts and minds of his disciples'. Oops!

Moreover, Christianity Lite is admittedly clueless as to what 'Christ will come again' might mean. Unbelievers, such as in Christianity Lite, have had nearly twenty centuries to think up a plausible counter-story for the Second Coming, to match the "hearts and minds of the faithful" counter-story for "Christ is risen.". If it is that difficult, it must be well nigh impossible. So maybe the Second Coming is as true (lower case 't') as the First Coming was. Watch! He may come back at any minute. Well, not quite any minute. The Bible implies that all peoples and tribes must have been told about Jesus and his salvation before he can come again, and that has not yet happened. So support the Wycliffe Bible Translators. They send linguistics specialists to remote tribes whose languages have not yet been transcribed, and so the gospel message has not yet been translated into their language. These Wycliffe missionaries take years living with the tribe, so they can understand the language and tell them the Good News that Jesus is their Lord and Savior. He instructed his disciples (us) to tell this good news in Judea and Samaria and to the ends of the earth. (Acts 1.8)

Meanwhile, many high profile leaders in main line Christian churches today assure the world that Jesus is not anything very special—salvation is just as accessible by hanging onto the coattails of Mohamed, or Joseph Smith, or Madame Blavatsky. I ask your prayers for the souls of the benighted. If you meet up with anyone trying to persuade you to any beliefs except that spelled out in the Nicene Creed, tell them, "That's mere vanity, and it isn't Christianity."

The overarching issue here is "Who is Jesus?" or as he himself put it, "Who do you say that I am?" The correct answer is the one given by the impetuous but ultimately authoritative Simon Peter: "You are the Christ, the Son of the Living God." Answering it this way may (or may not) be the ticket into Heaven.

Of course, we could be wrong about who is eligible. God may have all sorts of heavens. After all, Jesus says, "My father's house has many rooms." Perhaps there a Christian one, a Jewish one, a Buddhist one, an Islamic one, and so on. Maybe Hell is finding someone in Heaven you were certain deserved otherwise. Maybe Islamic Hell for Khalid Sheikh Mohammad is finding Danny Perl in Heaven, resting in the bosom of Abraham, when you were certain that torturing and beheading him in front of a camera was your ticket to Paradise with that bevvy of virgins. Judgmentalists, beware!

So I leave open the possibility that saving faith in Jesus Christ and Him Crucified is not all it's cracked up to be. The heaven it gets us may not be as exclusive as has been claimed. Given the overwhelming odds, though, why would anyone want to bet against the Triune God: Father, Jesus Christ, and Holy Spirit?

Because Christianity is so distasteful.

Fair enough. I know just what you mean. I find some versions of Christianity distasteful, too. But some of the versions I find distasteful turn out not to be genuine Christianity, after all. Some distasteful ones are indeed genuine—they believe the tenets of the creeds, even it they don't recite a creed in church—but they still may not be to my personal taste. It is usually a matter of cultural background or worship style that I object to—I don't like the music, or the way it is performed, or the minister's robes are grubby, or they have tacky plaster statues, or whatever. With a little self-discipline (and a lot of grace), I can get over it. Theology should trump cultural differences. Belief in and understanding of God's sovereignty trumps academic degrees, money, breeding, taste, and political connections. Not everyone who considers himself to be a Christian believes what a Christian is supposed to believe.

Theological understanding is no respecter of persons. On the contrary. Many highly educated people these days have come to belief in the sovereignty of God. Unlike when I was a philosophy student, philosophy and mathematics departments are hotbeds of Christianity. Well, perhaps that is putting it a bit strongly, but there are indeed now Christian believers in such places. In spite of this, though, many people in our society today don't have a close acquaintance with any genuine Christian Believers. The "Christians" they think they know are parodies of Christianity on TV. They don't know any middle-class, educated people who live in nice neighborhoods, and take their children to piano and horseback lessons, and sit there at field hockey games cheering for their daughters, and at wrestling matches cheering for their sons, and yet who go to church on Sunday mornings instead of to the gym. They don't know anyone who goes to a Bible Study during the week, and nurtures their toddlers with Godly Play.

They should get to know some real, honest-to-goodness Christians. Home-schooled students are the winners of many of the spelling, history, and geography bees, and similar contests in math and science, because their education beats what they would get in the public schools hands down. Another educational winner is a Classical Christian school, where the students learn Latin and Greek, and the classical literatures, and maybe biblical Hebrew as well. Graduates of such schools are also well-grounded in math and the sciences, and are among the best educated in our American culture today.

There was a time, not very long ago, when "Christians" put one another to death in the name of Christ. Inquisitors burned one another's adherents at the stake, hanged them, beheaded them, and claimed that it was on behalf of their faith in Christ that they were killing those whose faith was slightly different from their own. In Ireland, the Roman Catholics and the Protestant Christians were killing one another on behalf of the Triune God. How odd. How unchristian.

Anyone who does this in the name of Jesus has a false faith.—not Christianity. Jesus is very clear: the only way is the way of love. He says, "love your enemies, pray for those persecuting you, so that you become sons of your father in Heaven." (*Matthew* 5. 44-5) To kill someone for the sake of the gospel would be to heap burning coals upon one's own head. Paul says,

> Bless those persecuting you. ... live in peace with all men as much as you can, not avenging yourselves, beloved, but avoid their wrath, for it is written, 'Vengeance is mine, I will repay, says the Lord.' But if your enemy is hungry, feed him; if he is thirsty, give him drink ... conquer the evil with good. (*Romans* 12:14-21)

Given this, can we imagine that Jesus or Paul would have condoned Christians persecuting Jews or Protestants, or anyone else, for that matter?

If you are reluctant to try Christianity because you are put off by Christians, make sure those Christians are not fictional—in a play, on TV, in a movie. And make sure that those people are not in some weird sect, or just Christianity Lite. Get to know some real Christians. You might like them.

Remember our plight in Cherbourg without a map? Fortunately, the sun just happened to rise in the east that morning. Put the sun at our left and we are headed south! The sun rises in our lives, too. I can see clearly, now the dark is gone.

Lord, we believe. Help thou our unbelief.

14.
God, Our Vinedresser

Jesus says,
I am the true vine, and my father is the vinedresser.
He trims away every branch in me
that does not bear fruit, so that the vine
may bear more fruit.
Live in me, and I will stay with you.
The branch cannot bear fruit unless it
lives in me.

John 15:1-4 (loosely)

Now that it's daybreak, we must ask the Lord to guide us to the Christian community—i.e., a local church—where he wants us to be with him at that particular time. We can make no progress in Christianity outside of a Christian community.

A man had lapsed in his church attendance, when his pastor made a house call. Sitting in front of the fire, they had a conversation about his lack of week-to-week and day-to-day involvement in the church community. The clergyman quietly took the fire tongs, removed one brightly burning ember from the fire and put it on hearth, away from the rest of the fire. It smoldered, and went cold. The parishioner understood the message. He was in church the following Sunday, and became active in parish activities. Other benefits followed.

Jesus talks about the Christian community as a grape vine: "I am the vine, you are the branches. Stay connected to me, and your life will bear fruit. Apart from me, you can accomplish nothing (nothing good, that is)." (*John* 15:5)

The Church is the vine, the body of Christ in the world. We must connect. If we try to do anything good on our own, not connected to the vine, we will wither and die (perhaps becoming poison ivy in the meanwhile). Jesus didn't make this up: seven hundred years earlier, Isaiah had told us that all our works are as filthy rags. So we must try to find a church (a local expression of the Body of Christ) and get connected to the vine. We must go to church and Sunday school on Sundays, Wednesday night suppers and classes, whatever else they do.

Watching Christian television doesn't count, even when we send money and place our hands on the TV set for healing. Perhaps especially then.

We must find a real, actual church, and we must be sure that the church we find ourselves in is Bible-centered. We must be sure that great gulps of the Bible are read in church on Sundays, not merely the few verses the preacher has selected for the headline of his sermon, and that the sermon after the readings is an exposition of the Bible passage. If the sermon is not Bible based, we are probably in the wrong church.

How about the songs or hymns that they sing? These also should be chosen to reinforce that day's lesson from the Bible. Why the Bible? Why not some other great literature, or something contemporary that speaks to what is happening in the world today? Because the Bible is God's most direct way to communicate with us.

Does anybody think a super-intelligence like God couldn't find a way to communicate with his creation? He inspired people to write what we now call the Bible—the Holy Scriptures.

The Bible is not just an antiquated old document that is out-moded and out-dated and is not for our modern times. It **does** speak to what's happening in the world today—and in our life today. That is one of God's miracles. He is outside of space/time, and he knows and miraculously coordinates everything that is inside of space/time. So he caused all Holy Scriptures to be written for our learning. He wants us so to hear them: to read, mark, learn, and inwardly digest them, so that we may embrace and ever hold fast the blessed hope of everlasting life which he has given us in his Son our Savior Jesus Christ, who lives and reigns with him and the Holy Spirit, one God, forever and ever. (I didn't make that up; it is paraphrased from the Prayer Book.)

As I was saying … The public Scripture readings in church are planned ahead, in some cases hundreds of years ahead, to be read in the church or wherever you are, to apply to some particular situation in your life. If the local church where you find yourself (invited by a friend, or wandered there on your own off the street) is not Bible-centered, shake the dust of it off your shoes and move on, until you find one where …

- Scripture and the Lord's Table are the joint focus on Sundays.
- The Scripture passages are not selected ad hoc by the preacher and spun in a way that might apply to some bee-in-his-bonnet, but instead

are appointed ahead of time by some faithful authority to which he is beholden.

- Preaching is based on the Scripture passages; it expands on what the original context was, how those passages speak to us today, and the sermon itself is not dry as dandruff.

- Congregation is more like a stew than a bisque: mixed, not homogeneous. Old people and young, mixed races and ethnicities, rich and poor, sophisticated and salt-of-the-earth— each contributing to the flavor.

- Music also follows the Scripture passage, and is performed with excellence—as is everything else about the church. If it is done for the Lord, it should be done carefully and as well as can be done.[22]

- We should all have Holy Communion regularly. We take bread and wine together as a reenactment of Jesus' last meal with his disciples. He told them that the bread is his body, and the wine his blood. "Take this as often as you shall eat and drink it in memory of me." It is a meaningful rite.

- The people welcome us. If God doesn't want us to stay there, He makes us invisible, so no one will greet us or talk to us. Or he surrounds us with other visitors, who wonder why we don't greet them.

- We are at home, in spite of the strange things they do such as kneeling, or responding

---

[22] Anyone who says that we are wasting money when we spend on beautifying the church has the mind-set of Judas Iscariot. (John 12:2-6) And that is not a good thing.

together to things said, singing unfamiliar music, bowing, and otherwise doing things that I'm not used to.

Most Christians remember what it is like to be an unbeliever. The unbeliever is now trying to find out what it is like to be a believer. They should try being Rice Christians, and back it up with lots of prayer, lots of Bible reading. They need a Christian Bible, cheap at used book stores. How should we start reading the Bible? Where to begin?

If we are Jewish, we should start with *Matthew*'s gospel and *Acts*, and if we are not Jewish, we should start with *Luke'* gospel and *Acts*. We should all also dip into the Psalms. We should read some of each every day, but not force ourselves to read more than we want. Lots of people are amazed to find it interesting. For some people, the Bible is a real page-turner. Surprise, surprise! It is good to mark particularly meaningful snippets of the Bible to memorize. Even the shortest verse in the Bible—"Jesus wept" (John 11:35)—is full of God's self-disclosure: Who is this Jesus who could work miracles, who is the Second Person of the Godhead, and yet he is so human that he is standing there bawling his eyes out when his friend dies? The Lord helps us make pieces of his Scripture part of our very being, and they will stand us in good stead. We must put on the whole armor of God. (*Ephesians* 6.11f) Because …

… as we grow in our faith, Satan will begin to look at us as juicy morsels. He wasn't particularly interested in us back when we were denizens of his dominion. But now that we consider defecting to the other side, he suddenly finds us very attractive, and will tempt us cunningly. Watch out! Our best defense against him is to resist him and flee into the safety of a good church, which the Lord will provide. Satan's most wily guile is to persuade us to believe he doesn't exist.

We need not count on our local church for all of our training in Scripture. If he wants us to grow faster than our local church can bring us, the Lord will guide us to other training. This might be in another church—I have gone to another church's weekly Bible study for more than a decade or two—or it might be in the Bible Study Fellowship, which is an excellent nearly world-wide program for growth. For women it might be a Beth Moore Bible Study. University students will find growth by joining InterVarsity Christian Fellowship. The Lord will lead us to what we need.

So we have found a good church. Now we can relax and stay in that church, giving them our moral support, volunteer time, and a tithe of what the Lord gives us. What is a tithe? It's not a formula such as "one-tenth of your after-tax income". It is what we give back to the Lord, by giving it to our church. It includes some of the money the Lord gives us, some of the talent he gives us, some of our work, some of our leisure, some of our worldly goods, and so on. Some would call it pay-back time. We can give only some of what he has already given us—we have nothing else except what he has given us. As to the tithe amount we should pray about it. It may sometimes be very little, sometimes what seems like a princely sum, for a season. It should be significant to the tither, and the exact amount is between the tither and the Lord.

As we mature, God will give us many exercises in patience, and He'll use our time and resources in miracles for others. We must recognize growth, and be thankful that when that stage in our growth in faith comes, we will rejoice just as much for being used, as we rejoiced in being provided for in our theological infancy. Always, though, especially in the trials of our maturity, there is joy: joy in our fellowship with Jesus, and joy in our fellowship and mutual support of one another. Also we must remember that **always** all that we need, His hand will provide. The operant word here is 'need', not 'want' or 'wish for' or 'could use', and certainly not 'name and claim'. Sometimes he provides unimagined luxuries we couldn't have thought to ask for. Great is His faithfulness.

It's good to church-*shop* to find a good church. We shouldn't just assume that the one where we grew up is where he wants us. Once we have found one, we shouldn't church-*hop*, switching churches every time we feel slighted or not appreciated. (The eleventh commandment is, "Thou shalt not be disgruntled." The Hebrew original is, "Thou shalt not kvetch.") The Lord appreciates our efforts, even when we feel like nobody else does. And he's the one who counts, anyway. He is egging us on so he can make our efforts more fruitful. He promises to guide us into all Truth—but we mustn't assume that therefore we are automatically infallible. He teaches us through one another. And He won't be finished working on us this side of Heaven.

We live our lives before an audience of One. He is not located physically in one place. He is transcendent (beyond space and time), immanent (upholding the universe), incarnate (as the Son, born into human history), indivisible (without parts), omnipotent (there is nothing greater than himself that could cause him to suffer), eternal (without beginning or end), unlimited in power, wisdom and goodness, holy and righteous altogether. In Him there is no evil—no darkness at all. And he cares so much about his friends, and us among them, that he weeps for us.[xxxix]

The most important thing that has ever happened in the whole history of the world is His dying for our sins. The word 'sin' is not politically correct these days. Just as the Victorians did not speak of certain body parts such as legs (except already prepared by the cook and on the table)—the Victorians did not show ankle, and certainly not calf or knee. They were there, but were neither seen nor mentioned. Today we are equally fastidious about sin. We circumlocute by saying that bad things happen. But we do not say that someone sinned, to make these bad things happen. The sin is there, but we don't call it by its name. The difference between Victorian ankles and Postmodern sin is that the ankles were neither spoken of nor seen. The sin, however unspoken, is very much seen, front and center. It is flaunted. Our sin separates us from God. But we don't speak of it as sin.

Because our joy is contingent on loving what God loves, our sin separates us from joy. Remember? We pray, "Grant that we may love that which Thou ordaineth." Joy is the answer to that prayer. This joy is in loving what God loves. So in order to make us right with God and his justice, Jesus atoned for our sin, and our sins.

What does that mean?

We were created to love God and worship Him forever. But we allow sin to permeate our lives, so we turn away from loving God, and gravitate toward things that separate us from God. We are sinful by nature. But God loves his creatures so much that He came after us, like a mother running to keep her toddler out of the traffic. God came to us as the Son, the Second Person of the Trinity, the One God in Three Persons: Jesus, to show us how to live so as to be in right relationship with the Creator. That meant teaching us by example how to be fully human—to live in constant communication with God through prayer.

And then it meant taking our sin onto himself and dying in our place—sin that would otherwise condemn us to eternal separation from God and everlasting death and punishment. He took the punishment we deserve, so that we can live forever with him, worshiping him as we were created to do. In order for us to do this, He has to make radical changes in us.

Think of it this way: He changes us from pigs to lambs. Think of our sinful ways as mud – as nastiness that keeps us from being human in the best sense of the word. Pigs like to wallow in mud for cool and warmth. We wallow in our little piggy sins. Our "little" sins have fond, cute names—*péchée mignon; peccadillo; I made a boo-boo; oops! my bad*: for making fun of an old lady behind her back, or cheating just a wee bit on speeding or on political questionaires. Our piggy sins, which we from time to time most grievously commit, collectively inoculate us from any distaste of the hoggy sins to which we graduate: not just making fun of others, but putting electric probes at various places on their bodies, pulling out their fingernails, their eyes – such exquisite pleasures for hogs who have progressed to wallowing in *péchées majeures*.

Note to parents: We should never try to make our children good by telling them that sin is unpleasant. It is not: It is very pleasant, which is the reason people sin.
The German poet Heinrich Heine is quoted as saying, "I love to sin, and God loves to forgive. It is an admirable arrangement." No, Heinrich, and your characterization of it this way is a serious blunder.Sin is a seriously fun activity. It is not unpleasant at the time, but sin *leads* to unpleasantness, and then sometimes only after death.[xl] You've no doubt heard of people who died in the course of adulterous *flagrante delicto*. Their buddies probably thought, "What a way to go!" Little do they know. St. Peter probably tells them, "Go straight to Hell. Do not pass Go, do not collect $200." Eternity is a long, l-o-n-g time to be utterly and unredeemedly miserable.

Not everyone degenerates into hoggy sins of torturing others willfully. Some of us sin by being so self-centered that we pay no attention to the discomfort of others. But in the extreme, some people get quasi-sexual thrills from bullying other people. From torturing other people. Torture chambers, I am told, have initiated some of the most advanced technology of mankind's development. Miraculously, the Lord changes us one by one, by taking pigs and hogs and turning them into lambs and sheep. We are made into muddy lambs—we still are stuck in sin--but we no longer wallow in it with gusto. We learn to hate it. Analogies break down, but you get the point.

The Lord reaches underneath Mrs. Harding's pillowcase and takes the trash out of our lives. God changes our very being, so that we no longer want to sin, but now want to change, to be rescued from our proclivity to wallow in our sin. Instead of patting myself on the back for witty repartée, I now hate my nasty response to my spouse. I pray that I learn to hold my tongue.

If Jesus were not the divine Son, his execution at the hands of the Romans would not atone for our sins, and would not accomplish our salvation. It was by our hands that He was crucified, and at the same time, it was for us that He died.[xli] The Triune God is by nature a relationship of love within himself. The Father and the Son and the Spirit live in an eternity of divine love. God's decision to create the universe flows from the fullness and richness of His triune life, and not from any need or lack. Therefore we are made in and for a relationship with God and with one another.

Submission and subordination are honored in the life of the Trinity. The Father lovingly sends the Son. The Son willingly submits in love, rejoices to obey, and sends the Spirit. The Spirit lovingly points us to the Father and the Son, like a consummate art historian lovingly points us to the works of art in a museum, pointing out things in the painting we wouldn't otherwise have noticed or recognized or understood, explaining what they mean, and how the artist's brush strokes achieved the result. Or like a consummate jurist lovingly points us to the constitution and the legal code, explaining them and opening them up to our understanding, appreciation, admiration, and obedience. The self-disclosure of the living God is somewhat like the self-disclosure of a magnificent piece of music. It manifests itself, complete, unified, indivisible.

God's insistence that we worship Him is not the selfishness of a depraved husband who beats his wife and children into submission to him. It is the complete perfection of the Creator, who makes his creatures not into automatons, but into objects that are animated— that have souls. His creatures are somewhat like subway cars that seem from outward appearances to be complete when they come out of the factory, but they are not truly completed until they come in contact with the third rail, which empowers them to do the work they are made for—to run along the track.

God's creatures are more complex than the subway car. The subway car has no sense of incompleteness before its third rail encounter, whereas his creatures can think, can imagine, can want, can admire, can purpose to do things, and then do them. Or not. His creatures seek their own completion, but they get it wrong. They always get it not quite right until they find their own unique way to loving and worshiping the Creator.

Like a compass magnet is restless until it is oriented to the earth's magnetic field; like a sunflower is restless until it points its face to the sun: His creatures' hearts are restless until they find their rest in him. It is not until we are properly oriented with the creator that we can begin to be participants in his creation. By worshipping him and living within this orientation we participate in the construction of the Kingdom of God.

God's perfection demands our worship like a good meal demands a hungry tummy, a drink of wet water demands a parched tongue, a hot shower and a clean pillow demand an exhausted body. If that sounds backward, think about it.

It is this interactive God that the atheist rejects—always giving his creatures intellect and power, prodding us to make his creation whole and perfect. Is the atheist's rejection justifiable? No, it is an ontological short circuit: a short circuit in the atheist's analysis of what exists. That is the God whom Pascal urges us to bet on. And he assures us that we will be much the better for wagering on God. The rewards of saving faith are wondrous indeed, but possibly not the sort of thing that an unbeliever would think was anything worth striving for. As I said earlier, it's an acquired taste. But it's a French Truffle of a taste— magnificent, and expensive.

The intentional beauty of the worship environment is not made more beautiful the more money that is spent on it—that idea reminds me of the rococo churches in Europe, where the lavish gold and bovine-eyed murals are so not-to-my-taste that I find them worse than distracting. (How did the same culture come up with such tasteful music?) But on the other hand, the money should not be stinted. In making beauty for Jesus, a worshipful community offers the best they have, in monetary cost, in physical and artistic effort, and in good taste.

Those officiating in worship wear clothes, or vestments, appropriate to their office, well kept and laundered. The flowers are fresh and tastefully arranged, even when they are only greenery. The music is carefully rehearsed, by well-trained musicians, on the best quality instrumemts afforded. The people are welcome in whatever they wear, but as they mature they wear the best they have. This does not, of course, mean wearing a ball gown to church. It means honoring him by learning what apparel is most appropriate to the occasion, and wearing it gracefully.

Everything decently and in good order. And watch out! Here comes the joy!

Lord, we believe. Help thou our unbelief.

15.
We Get What We Want

Contrary to the Rolling Stones,
*we **can** always get what we want.*
And in the long run, we always do,
as far as God is concerned.
And he is always concerned.

"Who is God, anyway? Why should we elect him God?"

"I think he is just a selfish bore who wants everybody to praise and worship Him. Hah! What makes him deserve our praise, anyway? What has he done for us? Why should He get to say who can go to Heaven or Hell?"

"I want a god who will do what I want him to do, not a god who chooses to send some people to Hell."

"And Heaven shouldn't be just praising him, it should be having a good time. We deserve a good time, after all this hell on earth. I tell you this: I don't want to have anything to do with a Heaven that is nothing but praising God. I don't want to have anything to do with a God that just wants to sit there and be praised."

When the roll is called up yonder, some of us won't be there. But neither will anybody be banging on the pearly gates clamoring to get in. It is obvious that there are lots of people who have no desire at all to be in the presence of God for all eternity.

The Bible and Near Death Experiences and C.S. Lewis's *Great Divorce* give us a pretty good idea of what

Heaven is like, and it is an acquired taste. Lots of people have no intention of acquiring it. They don't want to have anything to do with God. And Heaven has everything to do with God. So they will be given their heart's desire. They won't go to Heaven when they die.

The psalmist says that they don't like blessing, and it will stay far from them (Psalm 109: 17) If they hate the Lord, they will get precisely what they ask for: They will be separated from God throughout all eternity. They will be as far away from Heaven and the presence of God as they can get. By choice.

Oh, they may decide that they have made a mistake, and say, "Oh-my-god! I goofed!!" But their cry will not be to the Lord of Heaven. They have used his name casually myriad times. They text it, they tweet it, they email it, they say it. But it is always dry on their lips. They have no idea of "Oh, my God! Help me, for I have sinned." No. "Oh-my-god" or "omg" is as far from "Oh, my God!" as the east is from the west. They will still desire to be that far from God. Their only regrets will be that is no golf or sex or booze or clever, scintillating conversation in Hell. They will still have no desire to acquire a taste for Heaven.

So in spite of the Rolling Stones, who sing, "You can't always get what you want," sometimes—at possibly the most important moment of our life—we can indeed get precisely what we want. In fact, we will all always get what we want when we die.

But that is not always a pleasant prospect. God is God. Every instant of the universe is both at his bidding, and caused by his immediate creation of it. Actually, he seems to handle it pretty well—as if he could do it forever, with one hand tied behind his back.

But if he were to stop doing it—to stop creating the universe, quit speaking it into existence—the universe would cease to be.

> This is the way the world ends,
> this is the way the world ends,
> this is the way the world ends,
> not with a bang, or even a whimper.
> Just . . . pfff!
>> (With apologies to T.S. Eliot)

Silence. Gone. Absolute nothingness, from our point of view, pfff . . .

But God himself won't go 'pfff': "Heaven and earth will pass away, but the Lord's words *(logoi[23])* remain." (Matthew 24:34) This is the God that some fools want to bet against. Little do they know: The game has already been decided, and God has won. Not with a bang or a whimper, but with a shout of triumph, he has defeated evil and death, and the souls of the faithful are resting in Abraham's bosom.

Heaven and earth will pass away, according to physicists and according to Jesus. But the Logos will remain: the words and logic and rationality, in 10^{500}

---

[23] For a discussion on the broader use of this term in the New Testament, please see my forthcoming volume, *Hiding in Plain Sight.*

string theories and in the mathematics of God, manifested in galaxies and gluons, the Logos who visited human history in the person of Jesus of Nazareth, the Logos will remain.

Pascal says,

> What harm will come to you from choosing this course? ... It is true you will not enjoy noxious pleasures, but will you not have others?

> I tell you that you will gain even in this life and that at every step you take along this road you will see that your gain is to realize that you have wagered on something certain and infinite for which you have paid nothing.[xlii]

The reader will note that we have reached the same conclusion as Pascal. Whether or not God exists, the benefits of betting on him are the same from having a saving faith in him:

- o If God exists, and we bet that he exists, he gives us saving faith. (Or we bet on him because he has given us the gift of saving faith. Chicken and egg.) We have joy on earth and Heavenly bliss for eternity. And after going to church Sunday morning to sing hymns and hear scripture and listen to it expounded in a sermon, and praying together and singing a few more hymns, we are well-rehearsed for the heavenly choir when we get there.

- o If God does not exist, we should still bet that he does. We concluded earlier that we must have instructions in our DNA such that if we bet on God, these instructions give us the joy in this life that we had erroneously attributed to the God who turned out not to exist. The same or a linked DNA code apparently also, as we die, would give us an endless dream that mimics the Christian version of Heaven.

Please remember, however, that this train of thought is suggested tongue in cheek. The author's serious hypothesis is that God exists, is sovereign, and we don't need to worry our feeble minds about it. Even without the DNA, we cannot lose by betting on God despite his hypothetical non-existence. We would still have the joyous phenomena—those are observable and testable, no matter what causes them.

As for the after-life in the case of a non-existent God, the most popular theory is that there is no after-life at all. There is just endless nothingness. The Near Death Experience evidence has pretty well knocked that theory into a cocked hat—except for the fact that anyone who believes it is so reluctant to give it up. If this hypothesis were true, it will be the same for those who bet for God and those who bet against him. So nothing would be lost by betting for or against him, and something stands to be gained by betting for him.

o The actual evidence at this time seems to indicate a penalty for betting against God in the form of a most unpleasant afterlife. We know this from hints of the 15% of Near Death Experiences that testify to a Hellish dream loop. The percentage of people who experience Hell may be much higher than the 15%, because of the many who cannot come back to tell about it, plus those who come back and chose not to tell about it.

So we would still win by betting for God. If he exists we win everything. If he does not exist, we lose nothing.

So, whether or not God exists, *if we bet that he exists* we get joy in this life. Whether or not he exists, if we bet on him we cannot lose. If he exists we get Heaven, because we want to spend eternity praising him. If he does not exist, we get an eternal pleasant dream, deluding ourselves that we are glorifying a God that unbeknownst to us is non-existent.

Similarly, whether or not God exists, *if we bet against his existence* we lose. We miss out on the joy in this life. And if he exists, then after we die we get his eternal judgment. If he doesn't exist, and we have bet against him, when we die we get nothingness disguised as an unpleasant dream.

In spite of overwhelming contrary evidence, some people will bet that he doesn't exist. It is not the job of believers to condemn others for not believing: Anyone has a God-given privilege to bet against God. We believers should instead seek every opportunity to be kind to them in every way we can, no matter that they disparage our faith. Think of it! If they are headed for Hell, any kindness we can give them may be the last kindness they will experience for all of eternity. Take them some soup, a pan of fudge, invite them to a movie, whatever you think might float their boat, because they are in danger of sinking.

But what do we know? We may be wrong about all this heaven and hell stuff—wrong in one of two ways.

First, we don't know who has achieved saving faith and who hasn't. It has not been given to us to know, and certainly not to decide, who goes to Heaven and who doesn't. So get over it!

Second, God may have prepared some kind of Heaven for each of us, whatever our belief system is. Who knows?

We should never despair over friends and loved ones we are afraid are lost. Yogi Berra was probably the one who observed that "It ain't over 'til it's over." Our unchurched friends might have a late-in-life conversion, and be there among those meeting us when we get to the pearly gates. Or they may be there to meet us because we Christians have wrongly assessed God's economy. Either way, let's give them the chocolate! They need the endorphins. And our prayers.

So. Do you agree? The rational move is to hedge by betting all we have on the Triune God's existence. We can't lose!

Lord, we believe. Help thou our unbelief.

Suggested Reading

William A. Dembski	*The Design Revolution*
God *&* Company	*The Bible*
Simon Greenleaf	*The Testimony of the Evangelists*
Timothy Keller	*The Reason for God*
Kenneth A. Kitchen	*The Reliability of the Old Testament*
C.S. Lewis	*Mere Christianity* *The Great Divorce*
Neil A. Manson	*God and Design: The Teleological Argument and Modern Science*
Mark Mittelberg	*The Reason Why Faith Makes Sense*
J.I. Packer	*Evangelism and the Sovereignty of God*
John Polkinghorne	*The Way the World Is* *The Faith of a Physicist*
John Stott	*Basic Christianity*
Lee Strobel	*The Case for a Creator*
N.T. Wright	*Simply Christian*

Index

Endnotes

[i] This is an endnote. Ignore them, except for finding out whose and what book the text is referring, and on what page.

[ii] N.T. Wright, *I Corinthians: 13 Studies for Individuals and Groups*, IVPConnect, 2009, 67

[iii] Isaac Asimov, *Smithsonian Institute Journal*, June, 1970, p 6

[iv] Blaise Pascal, *Pensees,* Translated by A.J. Drailsheimer, Penguin Books, 1966, "The Memorial", 309

[v] Baise Pascal, *Pemsées,* Series II, §418., Penguin edition, 152

[vi] C. FitzSimons Allison, *The Cruelty of Heresy,* (Harrisburg: Morehouse, 1994)161

[vii] Allison, *Heresy,* 166

[viii] Allison, *Heresy,* 164

[ix] Henry Allen, "The American Way of Eating", *The Wall Street Journal,* Saturday/Sunday, May 5-6, 2012, C5

[xix] Hannah Pylväinen, " 'Breaking Amish,' Burning Bridges", *The Wall Street Journal,* September 28, 2012, A15

[x] Jonathan Sacks, "Reversing the Decay of London Undone", *The Wall Street Journal,* August 21-22, 2011, C3

[xi] C.F. Allison, *Trust in an Age of Arrogance,* Cambridge, UK: The Lutterworth Press, 2011, 57-8

[xii] *World Magazine,* June 2, 2012, 12

[xii] Henry VanDyke (1852-1930 *The Hymnal 1982,* The Episcopal Church Pension Fund, 376

[xiii] James Martin, S.J., *Between He aven and Mirth: Why Joy, Humor, and Laughter are at the Heart of the Spiritual Life,* New York: HarperOne, 2011, 25

[xiv] Paul J. Zak, "The Trust Molecule", *The Wall Street Journal,* Saturday/Sunday, April 28-29, 2012, C1. See also his book from which this article is taken, *The Moral Molecule,* Dutton, May 2012

[xv] "Wiring the Brain, Literally, to Treat Stubborn Disorders", *The Wall Street Journal,* Tuesday, January 17, 2012, D2

[xvi] Daphne Merkin, "A Neurotic's Neurotic", *New York Times Magazine,* 30 December 2007

[xvii] C.F. Allison, *Arrogance,* 63

[xiii] John H. Rodgers, Jr., *Essential Truths for Christians*, (Blue Bell, PA: Classical Anglican Press, 2011) 141

[xix] John Gray, "notable and Quotable", *Wall Street Journal*, 19 Jan 2013, A-11.

[xix] Hannah Pylväinen, " 'Breaking Amish,' Burning Bridges", *The Wall Street Journal*, September 28, 2012, A15

[xix] Samuel Crossman, 1624-83, (Episcopal) *Hymnal 1982*, (New York: Church Pension Fund, 1985) #458

[xx] George Barna, *The Seven Faith Tribes*, (Tyndale House Publishers, Inc., 2009) 43

[xxi] *The Hymnal 1982, 100*

[xix] Hannah Pylväinen, " 'Breaking Amish,' Burning Bridges", *The Wall Street Journal*, September 28, 2012, A15

[xix] Peter Savodnik, "Their First Lenny Bruce Could Be Coming", *The New York Times Magazine*, May 27, 2012, 36

[xix] George Barna, *Seven Faith Tribes: Who They Are, What They Believe, and Why They Matter,* Barna: Tyndale House Publishers, Inc., 2009

[xxii] Pascal, *Pensees*

[xxiii] Johan Lehrer, "A Divine Way to Resist Temptation", *The Wall Street Journal*, May 12-13, 2012, C12

[xxiv] Martin, *Mirth*, 97

[xxv] Martin, *Mirth*, 221

[xxvi] Funk, "Twenty-one Theses", loc. cit.

[xxvii] Anthony Flew and Alasdair MacIntyre, *New Essays in Philosophical Theology*, New York: Macmillan, 1955, "Theology and Falsification: The University Discussion", 96-108

[xxviii] Lewis Carroll, *Alice in Wonderland*

[xxix] Pascal, §173, Penguin edition, 83

[xxx] John R. Polkinghorne, *Traffic in Truth: Exchanges Between Science and Theology*, Fortress Press, 2000.

[xxxi] Anthony Flew, "Theology and Falsification", 98

[xxxii] Finkelstein & Silberman, *The Bible Unearthed*, p. 34

[xxxiii] Roland de Vaux, *Ancient Israel, Vol. II*, 493

[xxxiv] Rodney Whitacre, *John*, (Downers Grove: InterVarsity Press, 1999) 54

[xxxv] John Rodgers, *Essential Truths*, 21ff

[xxxvi] Hampson, The Reverend James. This discussion thanks to his teaching to the Trinity Chapter, Daughters of the Holy Cross, St. Peter's Anglican Church, Tallahassee, January 2012.

[xxxvii] John Rodgers, *Essential Truths*, 95

xxxviii Pascal, *Pemsées,* Series II, §418, Penguin edition, 153

xxi Bernard Lewis, *Notes on a Century: Reflections of Middle East Historian,* Viking, 2012. 197-8

Made in the USA
Charleston, SC
03 March 2013